OTHER VOLUMES IN THIS SERIES

THE
BEST
AMERICAN
POETRY
1999

◇   ◇   ◇

Robert Bly, Editor

David Lehman, Series Editor

SCRIBNER

SCRIBNER
1230 Avenue of the Americas
New York, NY 10020

This book is a work of fiction. Names, characters, places, and incidents
either are products of the author's imagination or are used fictitiously.
Any resemblance to actual events or locales or persons, living or dead,
is entirely coincidental.

Set in Bembo

Manufactured in the United States of America

1   3   5   7   9   10   8   6   4   2

ISBN 0-684-84280-7
ISSN 1040-5763

CONTENTS

David Lehman was born in New York City in 1948. He is the author of four poetry books, including *Operation Memory* (Princeton, 1990) and *Valentine Place* (Scribner, 1996). *The Daily Mirror,* to be published by Scribner in January 2000, is a selection of the poems he has written since he began writing a poem a day as an experiment. *The Last Avant-Garde: The Making of the New York School of Poets,* his latest work of nonfiction, will appear in an Anchor paperback edition in October 1999. *The Perfect Murder,* his study of detective novels, is forthcoming in a revised paperback edition (Michigan). He has received a Guggenheim Fellowship in poetry, an Award in Literature from the American Academy of Arts and Letters, and a three-year writer's award from the Lila Wallace–Reader's Digest Fund. He is on the core faculty of the graduate writing programs at Bennington College and the New School for Social Research, and teaches a "Great Poems" course in the undergraduate honors program at New York University. He is the general editor of the University of Michigan Press's Poets on Poetry series. He initiated *The Best American Poetry* in 1988.

FOREWORD

by David Lehman

◇   ◇   ◇

"Not so long ago, the phrase 'California wine' belonged in the same book of oxymorons as, say, 'living poet' and 'Dutch cuisine.' You knew, on some level, that such things existed, but you didn't necessarily want any of them at your dinner table." Jay McInerney, who wrote these lines, thought them witty enough to serve as the lead of a *New Yorker* piece he recently wrote about California winemaker Robert Mondavi. The expulsion of poets from ideal republics is an old story, and what is most interesting in McInerney's formulation is the type of exclusion specified: the poet is barred from the socialite's banquet table, where French wine and French cuisine are served and conversation can be had with hip clever novelists, each a potential spokesperson for his or her generation.

Well, no one denies that poets receive fewer rewards than fiction writers. No poet can hope to enjoy as much fame, or as wide a readership, as a successful novelist. Even midlist fiction writers have a potential source of cash unavailable to the best poets, who waste little time praying that a Hollywood studio will take an option on their next book. (Martin Amis, in his recent story "Career Move," spins out the conceit, patently absurd, that sonnets are the vehicles of celebrity in our culture: "Don has a problem with the octet's first quatrain, Ron has a problem with the second quatrain, Jack and Jim have a problem with the first quatrain of the sestet, and I think we *all* have a problem with the final couplet.") Novelists are reviewed, moreover, while poets are largely ignored in the Sunday book supplements. Have a statistic. Between June 14, 1998, and September 27, 1998, five books of poetry were reviewed, and two others mentioned "in brief," in *The New York Times Book Review*. In the same period, ninety-six books of fiction were reviewed, with eighty-eight others treated "in brief." The ratio is even more comically one-sided when you factor in nonfiction books.

The irony is that American poetry today is not only, on its own terms, astonishingly vital and compelling, diverse and abundant, but also—though it is difficult to measure these things—probably in better shape altogether than contemporary American fiction. Indeed, the proliferation of memoirs written, in Oscar Wilde's words, "by people who have either entirely lost their memories, or have never done anything worth remembering," implies that narrative prose is stuck in that confessional box from which poetry moved on years ago. "But there is no competition," T. S. Eliot wrote in the biggest fib in his *Four Quartets*. "There is only the fight to recover what has been lost / And found and lost again and again."

Despite occasional reminders of its supposed second-class status, poetry today occupies a more honored place in the national consciousness than it has known since the 1960s, which was the last time in America that poets acted the part of heroes. The word *poetic* has long been an honorific when used to describe anything except poetry itself. (Example from the travel section: "In a corner of Lombardy, food is poetry.") But now poetry in the public imagination has acquired a dimension alien to the tradition of teacups and roses. In recent movies poetry is associated with liberation, truthtelling, and self-actualization. Life imitates *Bulworth* in which Warren Beatty, as a California senator running for reelection, sees the light and begins to tell it like it is—in the incessant rhymes and staccato rhythms of rap verse. In the movie's vocabulary the rapping ensures the speaker's authenticity and makes it possible for him to speak unpleasant truths in an insolent manner. (It may also signify the persistence of "the white negro" syndrome that Norman Mailer glamorized in an essay forty years ago). *Bulworth* didn't do as well at the box office as advance hype had projected, but it had its effect on politics. As Election Day 1998 approached, Vice President Gore, stumping for the Democrats, tried to shed his wooden image by rapping his election slogans. "We say, 'legislate'; the Republicans say, 'investigate.' " And, "We say, 'make the decisions'; they take depositions. / We know our future is nearing; they hold more hearings. / We say, 'heal our nation'; they just say, 'investigation.' "

In his book on Muhammad Ali, David Remnick reminds us that the great champion was the original rap artist and performance poet, who improvised his verses into microphones held by relentless interviewers. The fighter composed what Remnick calls, only half in jest, his "Song of Myself" before the bout with Sonny Liston in which he won the crown. He was still known as Cassius Clay then:

Now Clay swings with a right,
What a beautiful swing,
And the punch raises the bear
Clear out of the ring.

Liston is still rising
And the ref wears a frown,
For he can't start counting
Till Sonny comes down.

Now Liston disappears from view.
The crowd is getting frantic,
But our radar stations have picked him up,
He's somewhere over the Atlantic.

Before his fight with the aging Archie Moore in 1962, Clay predicted the outcome: "When you come to the fight, don't block the aisle and don't block the door. You will all go home after Round Four." In one of the more surprising sentences I encountered in 1998, I learned from Remnick that Moore had slipped easily into the role of the professorial critic, duly finding fault with the younger fighter's literary style. "Sometimes he sounds humorous, but sometimes he sounds like Ezra Pound's poetry," Moore said. "He's like a man who can write beautifully but doesn't know how to punctuate. He has this twentieth-century exuberance, but there's bitterness in him somewhere." True to his word, Clay knocked him out in the fourth round.

In 1999 Clay's verses would get more respect. Poetry today is celebrated and often appropriated in everything from the marketing of perfume to the ice dancing of former U.S. Olympic skater Kristi Yamaguchi, who has been doing a solo program set to ten love poems by Komachi and Shikabu, "women of the ancient Japanese court," in translations by Jane Hirshfield and Mariko Aaratani. Poetry has also been used to wage a kind of countercommercial campaign. In Los Angeles in January 1999 an outfit called Poets Anonymous spent roughly a million dollars to rent sixty billboards in prominent locations. For a month motorists were confronted with verse excerpts from a range of poets, including Pablo Neruda, Mark Strand, Charles Bukowski, and Lucille Clifton. I wondered what people made of the opening of Wallace Stevens's "The Well Dressed Man With a Beard," looming out at them at six major Los Angeles intersections: "After the final no there comes a yes / And on that yes the future world depends."

Bulworth isn't the only recent movie that capitalizes on the association of poetry with freedom, beauty, valor. *Life Is Beautiful,* Roberto Benigni's Oscar-winning movie, begins with a poet driving a car while declaiming verse. In his poem the brakes fail, and an instant later they do fail, and the car careens off the road, and it is this accident that brings the movie's hero and heroine together for the first time. (According to the New York *Daily News,* Benigni spent the afternoon preceding his Oscar triumph reading William Blake's poetry.) The greatly celebrated *Shakespeare in Love,* which won this year's Academy Awards for best picture and best actress, is an irresistible fantasy about the author of *Romeo and Juliet* and the romance that is said to have inspired him to write the play and, for good measure, the sonnet comparing the beloved to a summer day. "I love poetry above all," the beautiful heroine (Gwyneth Paltrow) tells Queen Elizabeth. The Swan of Avon himself cuts a dashing figure, adept at both lovemaking and derring-do; not only does he write poetry but speaks it as well, improvising as needed, no sweat. The coming attractions indicate that a new Hollywood production of *A Midsummer Night's Dream* is slated for summer release. A teen version of *The Taming of the Shrew*—renamed *Ten Things I Hate About You*—has just opened. Can a resurgence of Bardolatry be under way? It is April as I write this, and I have just watched a commercial for the Seattle Mariners. In the commercial the Mariners' shortstop reads the "quality of mercy" passage from *The Merchant of Venice* to the runner on second base. The distracted runner is then picked off. "The hidden Shakespeare trick," a Mariner in the dugout muses.

Entertainment Weekly—which reports that Bruce Springsteen is a "huge fan" of *The Best American Poetry* series—also reveals that the actor Charlie Sheen is a poet. Sheen reads from his work throughout a just-released straight-to-video movie, *Sisters:* "Did one depart with no remorse, / menstrual mood, unsigned divorce?" In one key respect Sheen is just like all other poets: he apparently failed to find a publisher for his manuscript when he completed it six years ago. Sultry songstress Jewel was luckier. *A Night Without Armor,* her first collection, was a pop sensation, with 300,000 copies in print. Critics invented new criteria to handle the phenomenon. "Jewel's book of poetry is solid by celeb-poet standards, and a fair bit of it is actually sort of readable in its own right," one noted. By mid-February 1999, *A Night Without Armor* had occupied a place on the *New York Times* bestseller list—where it was listed in Fiction—for nineteen weeks.

Poems are popping up all over the place. On the Internet, literary "zines" with names like *Nerve* and *Pif* are multiplying. A new development is the interactive poetry chat room. According to Robin Travis, who runs several such chat rooms out of her Alabama home, 100,000 poets visit her site every month. In the twenty-four-hour reading room, people present their poems for public reaction. Critical debate divides pretty evenly. "There are academics who trash everything," Travis says. "And then there are those who say, 'Awesome!' "

On television, poetry has been punctuating sitcoms and drama series. The title character of *Felicity*, a poetry-loving first-year student at a New York university, corresponds with an older, wiser friend, who advises her on matters of the heart. She quotes Auden: "If equal affection cannot be, / Let the more loving one be me." On *Sports Night*, which is set behind the scenes of a cable TV sports show, one of the anchormen caps a defense of yachting by quoting a dimly recollected poem about a sailor's yearning for "the lonely sky and the sea." The lines ring a bell, and the guys proceed to debate whether Whitman, Byron, Thoreau, Wordsworth, or Dylan Thomas wrote the poem in question—which turns out to be John Masefield's "Sea Fever" ("And all I ask is a windy day with the white clouds flying, / And the flung spray and the blown spume, and the seagulls crying.") A college student in *Party of Five* complains about having to write a term paper on Madonna's second album. "It's Emily Dickinson we need help with," she very sensibly says. In an episode of *ER* the new chief of the emergency room has made a career out of impersonating top professionals: an architect in the past, now a surgeon. She has fallen in love with one of the doctors. Exposed and expelled, she sends him a good-bye note with some highly erotic verses, as if she were their author: "Because two bodies, naked and entwined, / leap over time, they are invulnerable, / nothing can touch them, they return to the source. / There is no you, no I, no tomorrow." The doctor's pal recognizes the lines as from Octavio Paz's "Sunstone"—she is an impersonator as a poet, too.

The impulse to versify the Starr Report or President Clinton's videotaped testimony or Monica Lewinsky's taped table talk seized many writers in 1998 and '99. *Harper's* published Daniel Radosh's "Ode to Monica," consisting entirely of descriptions of her voice gleaned from daily newspapers in one month (Sample: "Rapid-fire ramblings, more Buffy than Bacall / Vulnerable, sympathetic, honest, small / Much younger than her 24 years / Heartbreakingly sad, pathetic, near tears / Smarter and more strident than expected / Not that of a Valley Girl bubble head / Dumb, Valley Girl, starstruck, adolescent, little girl, teeny-bopper.") In *The New Yorker,* Rick Moody constructed a verse collage ("She wanted to have sexual intercourse with him at least once / Call me but love and I'll be new baptized / She told me I looked fat in the dress") while John Updike, in "Country Music," sang of the girl in her "little black beret" who entranced the president and "led that creep astray." Monica Lewinsky disclosed that she had quoted *Romeo and Juliet* in a personal ad intended as an encrypted Valentine's Day appeal to her unnamed lover—a poignant detail. Bill Clinton turned to poetry in his most fulsome apology of the year, on December 11, quoting from Edward Fitzgerald's translation of *The Rubaiyat of Omar Khayyam* ("The moving finger writes; and having writ, / Moves on"). Maureen Dowd, impersonating the President in one of her columns, brings up the volume of *Leaves of Grass* that the commander-in-chief had given the intern. "We'll always have Whitman," Dowd has him saying. *Song of Myself* may not unseat *Casablanca* as the model for heartbreak romance. But you never know. It's gaining. As Ben in the TV show *Felicity* exclaims, "Whitman rocks."

It has reached the point that a hardnosed journalist can with a straight face declare—as Jim Adams does in *Esquire* (April 1999)—that poetry is the "next great nation-sweeping pop-cultural revolution" that "will follow the manly phenomena of cigars and steaks and martinis and leased luxury cars."

What accounts for the boom in poetry? The "leaves of grass-roots" populism goes back to Maya Angelou's inaugural ode in 1993 and the emergence, around the same time, of poetry slams and a vital "downtown" poetry scene. The university symposia continue, but these days there will also be festivals of cowboy balladeers, slammers, rappers, singing poets, railroad and hobo poets, stand-up improvisatory poets, and others—not to mention the free-versifiers, cutting-edge experimentalists, workshop veterans, and even traditional rhymesters who read their work in crowded smoky bars and chic cafés, some of which have the feel of speakeasies. New York residents have long grown used to waitpersons in fashionable restaurants who are actors in disguise. Now they may be poets as well. A friend and I were brunching recently at a Greenwich Village macrobiotic joint. When the French toast with warm fruit and soy links arrived, the waitress, overhearing our conversation, burst out, "Do you love poetry, too?" She went on to tell us that she had always loved poetry but that "it used to be a private thing. Now it feels more like a movement. Less scholastic and more visceral. More a part of my life." A few blocks away, at a Bleecker Street café, the guitarist in the rock band on his break approached the table where five poetry MFA candidates and their professor were discussing poetry. The guitarist said he'd just read a book by Rimbaud—he couldn't recall the title, because "it was in a different language, like French"—and asked if he could join the workshop.*

The aim of *The Best American Poetry* remains the greatest diversity consistent with the highest quality, with each year's edition serving as either a complement to or a corrective of any and all previous editions. The guest editor of this year's volume has had as lively a public career as any of his predecessors. Always outspoken, Robert Bly was a founder, in 1966, of American Writers Against the Vietnam War. He also fought against literary provincialism. He had discovered international modernism during a sojourn in Norway in the late 1950s. Upon his return to the United States he championed important European and South American poets (Neruda, Vallejo, Transtrømer, Machado), then all but unknown. Bly introduced a generation of poets to the possibilities of Surrealism—what he called "leaping poetry"—and the value of storytelling and myth in a laconic American idiom. His prose poems—"The Hockey Poem," for instance—gave that form a new legitimacy and currency. His charismatic readings were events. Bly might wear a primitive mask or accompany himself on a lyrelike instrument or otherwise violate decorum to strategic effect. No one present will soon forget the three lectures he delivered at Bennington College in January 1996. He would read us the poem he had written upon waking that morning, would lecture on the "reptilian" consciousness concealed in the layers of the human mind, and would coach us on "the bodily implications of the seven holy vowels."

With *Morning Poems* (1997), which struck me as his best volume in many years, Bly turned a corner. These "little adventures / In morning longing" address classic poetic subjects (childhood, the seasons, death, and heaven) in a way that capitalizes fully on the pun in the book's title. These are morning poems, full of the delight and mystery of waking in a new day, and they also do their share of mourning, elegizing the

---

*Translations, with the exception of self-translated poems, are ineligible for *The Best American Poetry*. This year Czeslaw Milosz's "A Ball" was deemed eligible, because it was not only written by him but translated by him (in collaboration with Robert Hass).

deceased and capturing "the moment of sorrow before creation." As I worked with Bly on *The Best American Poetry 1999,* I was struck by the range of his attentiveness—more than fifty magazines are represented here—and by his sustained commitment to a vision of poetry that he has done much to define. He has never lost the intense passion of allegiance to his favorite poets and to an "explosive" style, as he has termed it, in which "the power of the image comes forward as a form of thought."

The year this book commemorates was one of critical controversy. Of the several that spring to mind I would dwell for a moment on the case of Araki Yasusada: the poems purportedly written by a Japanese postal worker in Hiroshima who lost much of his family in the atomic blast of August 6, 1945. Putative translations of some of the poems, and of prose taken from the poet's posthumously unearthed notebooks, appeared to great acclaim in *American Poetry Review* three years ago and were later revealed to be a hoax, the handiwork of a poet named Kent Johnson, a professor at Highland Community College in Freeport, Illinois. *Doubled Flowering: From the Notebooks of Araki Yasusada,* containing the poems and some of the critical debate surrounding them (Roof Books, 1998), has extended this flamboyant, provocative, and incontrovertibly brilliant hoax.

It was not difficult to grasp why Johnson's complex creation incited tremendous passion. The hoaxer had, after all, masqueraded as a survivor of Hiroshima. Some thought this was in questionable taste or even, in the words of one offended magazine editor, a "criminal" act, a fabrication and a counterfeit exploitative of the victims of the first atomic bomb. Others were outraged by what they discerned as either racism or "white man's rage" in the writer's appropriation or imitation of Asian motifs. To his defenders the Yasusada poems and the whole elaborate apparatus of documents and inventions put into practice a clutch of crucial postmodernist notions and advanced critical theories. The hoax builds on Fernando Pessoa's example of inventing heteronyms and their poems; it put the "death of the author" hypothesis to an unexpected use in this constructed voice from beyond the grave. Was it a morally indefensible gesture or a daring avant-garde act in a jaded age that had given up on avant-garde ideals? Much depends on whether the value of the poems is textual and not dependent on information about the author or his method of work. One possible lesson of the hoax was stated by British writer Herbert Read in reference to Australia's Ern Malley poetry hoax in 1944. In the realm of ethics the ends rarely justify the means, Read observed. In the realm of art they always do.

This anthology series itself ignited controversy in 1998. In making the selections for *The Best of the Best American Poetry 1988–1997,* which was published last year, Harold Bloom chose none from the volume edited by Adrienne Rich in 1996. *Boston Review,* which a year earlier had given wide coverage to the Yasusada hoax, devoted a major portion of one issue to Bloom's essay and a major portion of the next issue to the responses it provoked from Marjorie Perloff, Rita Dove, Mark Doty, Thylias Moss, David Mura, J. D. McClatchy, Kevin Young, Donald Revell, Reginald Shepherd, Suzanne Gardinier, Ann Lauterbach, Carol Muske, and Sven Birkerts. I was sometimes asked to participate in or moderate debates centering on this battle of the books. Were these debates—hot-tempered and shrill as some were—a good thing, all in all? Was this controversy one more thing that you could defend on the grounds that it stimulated interest in poetry? I suppose I took some satisfaction in knowing that *The Best American Poetry* had served as the site for a clash of armies. Still, I couldn't help reflecting that this battlefield, like all others, was created with trees and grass and birds in mind and not dead soldiers.

Robert Bly was born in Minnesota in 1926. At Harvard (where his fellow undergraduates included Donald Hall, John Ashbery, and Adrienne Rich) he became poetry editor of the *Advocate* and edited a special issue marking T. S. Eliot's sixtieth birthday. In 1958 he launched *The Fifties,* and edited this influential literary magazine as it became *The Sixties* and briefly *The Seventies.* As an editor, translator, and teacher, he helped introduce a generation of Americans to great European and South American poets, such as Neruda, Vallejo, Transtrømer, and Machado, and to the possibilities of Surrealism, or "leaping poetry," as Bly called it. *The Light Around the Body,* his second collection, won the National Book Award for poetry in 1968. The men's movement in the United States owes a filial debt to this writer's imagination and to *Iron John* (1990) in particular. But Bly's dedication to poetry has always been paramount. His recent publications include *Morning Poems* (1997) and *Eating the Honey of Words* (HarperFlamingo, 1999), a volume of new and selected poems. In collaboration with Sunil Dutta, he has translated the poems of Ghalib from the Urdu under the title *The Lightning Should Have Fallen on Ghalib* (Ecco, 1999). Bly lectures widely. He lives with his wife in Minneapolis.

INTRODUCTION

by Robert Bly

◇ ◇ ◇

1.

After reading several hundred literary magazines offering both poetry and fiction this year, I have concluded that American poetry now is much more lively than American fiction. Seventy-five recent poems appear in this book. Many different kinds of *heat* show in the poetry collected here: heat of friendship (Robert Creeley), heat of wit (Carolyn Kizer), heat of the blues (Sonia Sanchez), heat of form (Richard Wilbur), heat from the subterranean caves (Russell Edson), heat of the hopeless brave fight against political hypocrisies (Lawrence Ferlinghetti, Hayden Carruth, John Haines), the heated defense of a great writer (Tony Hoagland on D. H. Lawrence), heat of the furious daughter (Molly Peacock), heat of the meadows and the hawks (Mary Oliver).

2.

Heat in itself has been disappearing for some years from our English. It is said that in a single day in the United States more words appear on computer screens than are secreted in all the books in the Library of Congress. But as these words stream across our screens, freed from doubt or elegance, we can see that computer verbiage has become the model of cool and empty language. I'm not making an original claim here; we all agree that the language of the chat rooms is empty. It's as if some worldwide force were trying to free us all from literary style, and is succeeding. Many contemporary writers persuade themselves it is good not to have inwardness, not to have intensity, not to engage layers of meaning, not to have pungent phrasings, not to allow the heat of that sort of language that springs from the fight between God and the donkey. It's possible that the particular heat which we call style amounts to recognizing and remembering the flavor of the decade in which one became an adult. We more and more have English now no longer stung by the mood of an Oklahoma afternoon in the thirties, or the flavor of an Illinois dusk in the forties. Hardy's language we recognize to be blessedly imprisoned in the mood of Sussex in 1880. When the irreplaceable flavor of a given decade disappears, our language loses its vigor and becomes merely useful. Sven Birkerts, in his new book of essays *Readings,* points directly to the decline of intensity that results from the shift from the page to the screen. "We are losing our grip, collectively, on the logic of complex utterance, on syntax; we are abandoning the rhythmic, poetic undercurrents of expression." He suggests that "postmodern" merely means the destruction of all style. Postmodern novelists have fallen headfirst into this release from period style, producing novels that contain only the melancholy emptiness that follows from the longing to become universal. When language cools, it becomes a corpse.

American poets are fighting against this cooling in several ingenious ways. Not all poets, of course. One group of poets who call themselves "Language" poets work very hard to drain all the meaning out of the words they use, and in this way resemble those eighteenth-century doctors who treated all problems by bleeding, occasionally failing to notice that the patient had died from loss of blood. All of us, poets, essayists, and fiction writers alike, are being pressured by example to remove flavor from our work, along with our idiosyncrasies. We are fighting a front-line action against the cooling of language, and that struggle is a theme of the remarks I'll make in this essay.

3.

I'd like to discuss some of the poems that appear in this book in relation to the mysterious quality of heat. One sort of heat we might call the heat of arrival, which we can contrast with the coolness of mediocre poetry that wanders among pages of reminiscences. Here is a fifteen-line poem by Ruth Stone:

> Across the highway a heron stands
> in the flooded field. It stands
> as if lost in thought, on one leg, careless,
> as if the field belongs to herons.
> The air is clear and quiet.

Snow melts on this second fair day.
Mother and daughter,
we sit in the parking lot
with doughnuts and coffee.
We are silent.
For a moment the wall between us
opens to the universe;
then closes.
And you go on saying
you do not want to repeat my life.

We can tell when a poem has *arrived* by a certain feeling in the gut, as if a dismaying thought had slipped past our defenses. We feel that something has been taken seriously enough that it has hurt the poet.

Hayden Carruth remembers one night in Chicago when the great jazz musician Sidney Bechet, having become disgusted with the white band, sat in front of them drinking ponies of brandy, then throwing the empty glasses at the trumpet player. Now that Carruth himself is older,

I see sparkling glass ponies come sailing at me
out of the reaches of the impermeable night.

Billy Collins wants to love his dog as a kind of Gandhi-like being free of attachment, but it doesn't work.

If only she were not so eager
for a rub behind the ears,
so acrobatic in her welcomes,
if only I were not her god.

Robert Creeley, thinking of Mitch Goodman's death, says:

. . . *Hold my hand, dear.*
I should have hugged him,
taken him up, held him,
in my arms. I should
have let him know I was here.

Jane Hirshfield's poem begins by recalling a small rat and a snake she once saw living together in her room. Her words travel well together, but the poem really arrives when she is able to acknowledge that she too has the snake and the rat inside her, as well as larger beasts:

> There are openings in our lives
> of which we know nothing.
>
> Through them
> the belled herds travel at will,
> long-legged and thirsty, covered with foreign dust.

Ernest Hemingway had several gardeners toward the end of his life, and David Ray, by a feat of marvelous storytelling in his poem, lets us feel the heat of the shotgun approaching closer and closer. David Ignatow's poem in this collection, written shortly before he died last year, we could call a masterpiece of arrival.

> The apple I held and bit into was for me. The friend who spoke to me was for me. My mother and father were for me. . . . The bed I slept in was for me. The clothes I wore were for me. The kindness I showed a dead bird one winter by placing it in my warm pocket was for me. . . . The music on the radio, the books I was beginning to read, were all for me.
>
> I had hold of a good thing, me, and I was going to give of my contentment to others, for me. . . . I had found that for me was everybody's way. . . . And so when I looked up at the night stars, for me remained silent, and when my grandmother died, for me became a little boy sent on an errand of candles to place at the foot and head of her coffin.

Ignatow puts an amazing amount of backward-looking heat into this little phrase "for me." Thomas R. Smith has been dreaming of the dead in his family:

> On Christmas Eve, I prepared a warm
> place for my mother and father, sister
> and brothers, grandparents, all my relatives,
> none dead, none missing, none angry
> with another, all coming through the woods.

Peggy Steele's father finally arrives to her when she imagines him as a ne'er-do-well who walks all night in a small town:

My father walked the night.
My father walked the night.
It seemed deeper than all Shakespeare.

Philip Levine wants to find his father as he drives along the old roads, but instead he arrives at "the stubbornness of things":

I took off my hat, a mistake in the presence
of my father's God, wiped my brow with what I had,
the back of my hand, and marveled at what was here:
nothing at all except the stubbornness of things.

4.

Richard Wilbur's brilliant new poem "This Pleasing Anxious Being" will make a good text to discuss another sort of heat: a heat that comes from making demands on language in such a way that the language fits into a prechosen form. Whitman achieved a heat by apparently abandoning the stanza form, though he is not abandoning that form so much as accepting a still older form that requires the rhythms of Biblical and operatic recitation. Richard Wilbur, like Frost, uses his strength to bend language, as if two wrestlers were fighting, and he refuses to release the wrestler until he feels the sinews under his fingers "like chords of deep music." In writing so, he remains faithful to the sting of the late 1940s and the pentameter line, which was a part of the flavor of those days. He chooses a few hours when his family are driving on the black roads of 1928, in a snowstorm, and he drives English into one of its possible animal gaits:

Wild, lashing snow, which thumps against the windshield
Like earth tossed down upon a coffin lid,
Half clogs the wipers, and our Buick yaws
On the black roads of 1928.
Father is driving; mother, leaning out,
Tracks with her flashlight beam the pavement's edge,
And we must weather hours more of storm
To be in Baltimore for Christmastime.

With his firmly disciplined stanzas, as in the beautifully modeled stanzas of Carolyn Kizer as well, we arrive at someplace far from us and yet holding inside itself the treasures of wit and human foolishness. In some poems the arrival takes the form of a feeling that some spiritual treasure, long hidden in the soul, has been found, as when a walker in the woods finds an old cup near an abandoned spring. Frost wrote: "Drink and be whole again beyond confusion."

5.

T. S. Eliot said:

> We have lingered in the chambers of the sea
> By sea-girls wreathed with seaweed red and brown
> Till human voices wake us, and we drown.

Two things strike me in this little passage. The first is the suggestion that twentieth-century mental life has cooled to the point that if a human voice should penetrate our verbal world, we would be so shocked that we would drown. That fear touches on the present coolness of language, which is increasingly psychic but not of the soul. The second word that moves me is *chambers*. We are lingering "in the chambers of the sea." I'd like to relate these rooms not so much to the sea as to rooms inside our heads that more and more interfere with our taking in the power of what we see.

We could dip first into the speculations of those experts who study the processes of perception. What happens when we see snow on the windshield or a black road? The falling snow—inverted, we are told—is not passed along directly to the soul, but first is sent through five mental chambers. In the first chamber, the dark and light of it is verified, the thickness or thinness of the snowfall is verified. Next we could say that the image of the snow is sent on to the chamber of memory, where our representatives compare it to all the other snowfalls we have seen. The compared image is then sent on to the chamber of intellect, which relates ideas to the image, and decides if it is a symbolic snowfall or a real snowfall. Our representatives in this chamber classify the incoming image as "Western" or "Eastern," "imperialistic" or "democratic," "hegemonic" or "okay." Perhaps for some, the image then moves out of the chamber of practical intellect to the chamber of spiritual intellect, that chamber "at the top of the stair" where St. Teresa and St. John spent "the whole fiery night." At any rate, the image finally approaches the chamber of the "I," a jealous chamber which may or may not pass the image on to the soul.

This visualization of chambers may strike some readers as arbitrary, even incorrect. Perhaps it is. My main thought is that we, in 1999, being so worldly, so informed, so flooded with motifs from the past, find it more and more difficult to allow any object, whether a snowstorm or a toad or a painting, to pass through our subtle chambers to reach the soul. Students in graduate school, even some poets, are taught to linger in these chambers of the mind until they decide to remain there, as "in some mid kingdom dark."

The job of the writer who knows about these chambers is to give us a frog or a giant or a snowstorm and to protect it from all the invisible forces that want to delay it, elaborate it, relate it to correct opinions, prevent it from arriving at the soul. We recognize that Rilke achieved in "The Panther" some protection like that for the panther he was watching in a zoo, so that it arrived at our soul still wild:

> The lithe swinging of that rhythmical easy stride
> which circles down to the tiniest hub
> is like a dance of energy around a point
> in which a great will stands stunned and numb.

Wallace Stevens wrote:

> I placed a jar in Tennessee,
> And round it was, upon a hill.
> It made the slovenly wilderness
> Surround that hill.
>
> The wilderness rose up to it,
> And sprawled around, no longer wild.
> The jar was round upon the ground
> And tall and of a port in air.
>
> It took dominion everywhere.
> The jar was gray and bare.
> It did not give of bird or bush
> Like nothing else in Tennessee.

This poem is a triumph in its capturing and retaining the heat of the jar. Twisting away from all philosophies, Stevens gives the jar to the soul. A painter's task is very different, but we recognize that Rembrandt is able to bring the wrinkled face of an old woman right up to our soul.

We have to ask: these pesty chambers, these rooms of verification, of classification, of comparison, of judgment, are these chambers noxious? Not at all. We could not be human without them. In fact, the ultimate purpose of our going to grade school, high school, and university is to elaborate and refine those chambers. Anyone who doesn't know the difference between the practical intellect's house and the spiritual intellect's house is doomed to be dragged over fields of sharp stones by idiots. Even the chamber of the "I," of which the Buddhists are rightfully suspicious, is a marvelous chamber, full of energy and sarcasm. So he or she who loves art and culture will honor all these Chambers of the Mind. But at the moment an artist is about to set down his or her poem, the wise artist will let them all go, bless them with gratitude and rejection, until nothing is left but the snowfall touching the soul. The greatest heat in a poem appears when the poet is able, by his or her awareness of complicated mental perceptions, to bypass those perceptions and bring the object just seen so near the soul that the soul feels a shock, as if it had just touched snow or hot water.

R. H. Blyth said that to experience a true haiku is akin to putting your hand into boiling water. He means that the haiku poet is sometimes able to remove all the intervening material so that the reader experiences the wind or the snow brushing directly on his or her own soul. The haiku is limited in length, of course, because no one wants to keep his or her hand in boiling water very long. It's perhaps foolish to present a haiku in translation, but we can get a little feeling of a Bashō haiku from his description of the winds around the old walking station on Mount Asama:

> Storm on Mount Asama!
> Wind blowing
> Out of the stones.

One of the poets in our collection who is not very well known, Franco Pagnucci, wrote this lovely poem about toads:

> Yesterday toads
> no bigger than houseflies

took small hops
across our path.

It would have been easy
to miss them—
under the tall trees and the charm
of the wind in their tops—
those perfectly shaped
little black toads
along the black path.

Sharon Olds's poem in this book, a poem whose mood is so new for her, achieves a comparable shock of perception.

. . . This morning, when I looked
at a lily, just beginning to open,
its long, slender pouch tipped
with soft, curling-back lips, and I could peek just
slightly in, and see the clasping
interior, the cache of pollen,
and smell the extreme sweetness, I thought they were
shyly saying Mary's body,
he came from the blossom of a woman, he was born
in the beauty of her lily.

David Wagoner's poem "Thoreau and the Crickets" also labors in this Bashō field. His poem describes field crickets lying embedded in the ice of a marsh. Wagoner's poem goes far past the length of a haiku, but he doesn't lose the crickets.

The genius of William Stafford lies in his ability to pass swiftly, magically through the chambers—which in his thought he honored so well—and so to bring the soul close up to the thing he is looking at. A month or so before he died, he wrote this poem:

At night outside it all moves or
almost moves—trees, grass,
touches of wind. The room you have
in the world is ready to change.
Clouds parade by, and stars in their
configurations. Birds from far

touch the fabric around them—you can
feel their wings move. Somewhere under
the earth it waits, that emanation
of all things. It breathes. It pulls you
slowly out through doors or windows
and you spread in the thin halo of night mist.

6.

This introduction is just about finished. I have used it to admire a
number of poets in this book, and I have praised the heat in current
American poetry, some of the heat given by arrival, some given by a
stubborn devotion to form, some by allowing the night mist to brush
up against the soul. It might be good to mention—as a complaint—a
form of heat which, though present in some European poetry, I find
missing in much American poetry now.

I'm referring to the poem that can be imagined as a series of tiny
explosions. I miss that sort of poem these days. At one time just after
World War II, we considered ourselves to be students of the great Euro-
pean culture, French, German, Italian. As a consequence, we translated
Ungaretti, Rilke, Montale, Vallejo, Neruda, Jiménez, Lorca, Akhma-
tova as one translates one's betters. American poets at that time
admired especially the way European poets like Montale or Rilke
would hide, without weakening it by explanation, a secret inside a
poem, so that when we begin to investigate the secret, we feel it as an
explosion. That explosiveness is distinct from, though not necessarily
better than, a more slow-burning poetry. An Ungaretti poem, in its
entirety, says:

> *M'illumino*
> *D'immenso.*

His poem is either two words or four words, depending on how you
count them. Let's try to translate it:

> Immensity fills
> Me with light.

Or:

>   My sun inside
>   Rises from space.

Or.

>   I pull in immense
>   Space and am in glory.

Or:

>   I light up my soul
>   With the hugeness of space.

But it's clear that the two "o's" of *illumino* and *immenso* are part of the explosion. How can we do that in the translation? Impossible. All we know is that when light and space are brought close to each other, they explode. Cesar Vallejo wrote:

> I will die in Paris, on a rainy day,
> on some day I can already remember.
> I will die in Paris—and I don't step aside—
> perhaps on a Thursday, as today is Thursday, in autumn.

Neruda provides one mysterious explosion after another, which we cannot participate in unless we are willing to create the wild image:

> Death is inside the bones
> like a barking where there are no dogs.

★　★　★

> It so happens I am sick of being a man.
> And it happens that I walk into tailorshops and movie houses
> dried up, waterproof, like a swan made of felt
> steering my way in a water of wombs and ashes.

The South American poets learned all that from Lorca, who had learned it from the Arabs.

It's possible that—as our pop culture dominates the globe—a certain national smugness affects us all, and that, as a result, the poets, subtly, without intending to do so, not noticing it, have stopped drawing their models from the great Europeans. This lack of tutoring has been a mistake, but one that we can correct. Jane Kenyon, with the help of Vera Dunham, apprenticed herself to Anna Akhmatova, and some classically deep American poetry came from that union.

I mention this "poetry of explosions" because I would like to urge some of our younger poets to try this way of writing. It is not an efficient way of writing. It uses up a lot of energy; a single line might absorb the energy which could have created a whole stanza. It takes tremendous stamina to write a page-long poem by the explosive method, so many poets prefer bulk achieved in a less exciting way.

The three poets in our book who best know how to do this are Russell Edson, Louis Jenkins, and Charles Simic. Russell Edson has a genius for this kind of little explosion:

> She had fallen in love with her doctor's stethoscope; the way it listened to her heart . . .

Louis Jenkins studies the wide-eyed gaze that cannot understand what it is looking at—the deer in the forest puzzled at what she sees, a pike examining a fishing lure.

> There isn't a way in the world I'd bite on that thing. But I might swim in just a little closer.

Charles Simic is always the European among us—he, too, tries to figure out what he sees:

> What the hell is going on here, I said?
> At which the barber rushed over
> And threw a hot towel over my eyes.

Something interesting happens when you place Jenkins's fishing lure next to Carolyn Kizer's poem. To St. Augustine and Kierkegaard, women were as mysterious as a fishing lure. So Carolyn Kizer, too, participates in the European poem with her wonderful brooding on the zany Europeans Kierkegaard and Augustine who couldn't understand what they were seeing either.

Having an opportunity to admire the different sorts of heat in contemporary American poetry has made me feel still more grateful to David Lehman, both for his inviting me to edit this selection, and for his persistent, driving support of the whole project. His book on deconstruction, *Signs of the Times,* first alerted me to his love of genuine literature; and he has been unfailingly generous and helpful in finding obscure magazines and recommending strange tomes one might never find on one's own.

In some cultures, the German for one, poetry has really never moved out of the university. However much we deplore our own excesses, we have a right to be proud of the hundreds and hundreds of poetry events, raucous poetry slams and quiet poetry readings that happen all over the United States. The intensity of the U.S. poetry scene is often astonishing; and the *Best American Poetry* series of collections, going back to 1988, is a strong part of that scene.

When James Laughlin, who was then just out of college, visited Ezra Pound and showed him some poems, Pound said, "Well, you won't get far with your poetry. Do you belong to the Laughlin steel mills family? My advice is to go home and start a publishing house." So Laughlin did. We'll end these notes with Laughlin's poem written when he notices, as he has grown older, how much he has not set down:

> Little time now
> and so much hasn't
> been put down as I
> should have done it.
> But does it matter?
> It's all been written
> so well by my betters,
> and what they wrote
> has been my joy.

This love of good poetry, no matter who has written it, is the real mood of literature.

The Selfishness of the Poetry Reader

◇   ◇   ◇

Sometimes I think I'm the only man in America
who reads poems
and who walks at night in the suburbs,
calling the moon names.

And I'm certain I'm the single man who owns
a house with bookshelves,
who drives to work without a CD player,
taking the long way, by the ocean breakers.

No one else, in all America,
quotes William Meredith verbatim,
cites Lowell over ham and eggs, and Levertov;
keeps *Antiworlds* and *Ariel* beside his bed.

Sometimes I think no other man alive
is changed by poetry, has fought
as utterly as I have over "Sunday Morning"
and vowed to love those difficult as Pound.

No one else has seen a luna moth
flutter over Iowa, or watched
a woman's hand lift rainbow trout from water,
and snow fall onto Minnesota farms.

This country wide, I'm the only man
who spends his money recklessly on thin
volumes unreviewed, enjoys
the long appraising look of check-out girls.

How could another in America know why
the laundry from a window laughs,
and how plums taste, and what an auto wreck
feels like—and craft?

I think that I'm the only man who speaks
of fur and limestone in one clotted breath;
for whom Anne Sexton plunged in Grimm; who can't
stop quoting haikus at some weekend guest.

The only man, in all America, who feeds
on something darker than his politics,
who writes in margins and who earmarks pages—
in all America, I am the only man.

from *The Café Review*

Story

◇   ◇   ◇

The guy picked me up north of Santa Fe
where the red hills, dotted with piñon,
loop down from the Divide into mesas and plain.
I was standing out there
—just me, my pack, and the gila monsters—
when he hauled his Buick off the road
in a sputter of cinders and dust.
And got out, a gray-bearded, 6-foot, 300-pounder,
who stretched and said, "Do you want to drive?"
So I drove and he told me the story of his life.
How his father was a Russian Jew
who got zapped by the Mob during Prohibition,
how he quit school at fifteen
and got a job as a DJ in Detroit,
how he sold flatware on the road and made a mint,
how he respected his wife, but didn't love her,
how he hit it big in radio and TV, how he fell in love,
how he found himself, at 50, in intensive care
with his wife, his kids, his girlfriend, and rabbi
huddled in silence about his bed
when his doctor came in and whispered
that maybe he ought to ask the wife,
and the girlfriend, to alternate visits
"because it wasn't too good for his heart."
"What about your kids?" I asked. "What do they do?"
"My daughter runs our store. My son is dead."
He studied the Rockies and didn't continue.
"What did he die of?"

"He died of suicide.
No, that's not right. . . . Nixon killed him.
My son was a sweet kid, hated guns and violence
and then, during that fucking war, he hijacked a plane
and flew it to Cuba. He shot himself in Havana."
He watched the road, then grinned and said,
"Brave little fucker, wasn't he?"

from *Verse*

Bill Matthews Coming Along (1942–1997)

◇ ◇ ◇

They say the best French wines have *terroir,* meaning the taste of the lay of the land that works through and gets held in the wine, the bouquet of a particular hillside and of the care of those who work there.

When I see Bill Matthews coming along, I see and taste the culture of the world, a lively city, a university campus during Christmas break, a few friendly straggling scholars and artists. I taste the delight of language and desire and music. I see a saint of the great impulse that takes us out at night, to the opera, to the ballgame, to a movie, to poetry, a bar of music, a bar of friends.

When I see Bill Matthews stopped at the end of a long hall, I see my soul waiting for me to catch up, patient, demanding, wanting truth no matter what, the goofiest joke, the work with words we're here to do, saying how it is with emptiness and changing love, and the unchanging. Now I see his two tall sons behind him.

Bill would not say it this way; he might even start softly humming *Amazing Grace* if I began my saying, but I go on anyway: god is little g, inside out, a transparency that drenches everything you help us notice: a red blouse, those black kids crossing Amsterdam, braving the cabs, a nun. You sweet theologian, you grew new names for god: gourmet, cleaning woman, jazz, spring snow.

What fineness and finesse. I love Bill Matthews, and I did not have *near* enough time walking along with him, talking books and ideas, or sitting down to drink the slant and tender face of Provence.

from *Figdust*

Catch

◊　◊　◊

My father came home with a new glove,
all tight stitches and unscuffed gold,
its deep pocket exhaling baseball,
signed by Mays, or Mantle, or The Man,
or some lesser god I've since forgotten.
He took off his tie and dark jacket
and we went outside to break it in,
throwing the ball back and forth
in the dusk, the big man sweating
already, grunting as he tried
to fire it at his son, who saw now,
for the first time, that his father
who loved to talk baseball at dinner
and let him stay up late to watch the fights
unfold like grainy nightmares
on Gillette's Cavalcade of Sports,
the massive father, who could lift him
high in the air with one hand,
threw like a girl—far and away
the worst we could say of anyone—
his off-kilter windup and release
like a raw confession, so naked
and helpless in the failing light
that thirty years later, still
feeling the ball's soft kiss in my glove,
I'm afraid to throw it back.

from *Sewanee Review*

Foreign-Domestic

◇　◇　◇

I listen to the sweet "eye-fee."
From where I'm sitting I can see
across the hallway in your room
two bare feet upon the bed,
arranged as if someone were dead
—a non-crusader on a tomb.
I get up, take a further look.
You're reading a "detective book,"

so that's all right. I settle back.
The needle in its destined track
stands true and from the daedal plate
an oboe starts to celebrate
escape from the violin's traps
a bit too easily perhaps
for twentieth-century taste, but then
Vivaldi pulls him down again.
Said Blake, "And mutual fear brings peace,
Till the selfish loves increase . . ."

from *Conjunctions*

Tired Sex

◇   ◇   ◇

Trying to strike a match in a matchbook
that has lain all winter under the woodpile:
damp sulfur
on sodden cardboard.
I catch myself yawning. Through the window
I watch that sparrow the cat
keeps batting around.

Like turning the pages of a book the teacher assigned—

You ought to read it, she said.
It's great literature.

from *The Atlantic Monthly*

Narrow Road, Presidents' Day

◇ ◇ ◇

As I drive by
the architect's
house, his wife's

just opening up
the sideyard window
and leaning out

on her elbows to
talk with three
backyard sheep.

She smells spring.
Given sun trying
to break through

dawn fog, fog after
all-night rain, on
top of two months

of old snow, she
gives herself
gasps of light.

Not a mile back,
just beyond Harman's
Farm Stand, all

boarded-up against
winter, almost at
the new place where

they sell Russian
tractors, I sniffed
skunk, first time

this year. Had to
swerve my pickup
to keep from side-

swiping the skunk,
already dead. And
next to him, for

Christ's sake, a big
mother porcupine,
dying hard.

I kept on driving
to work. I keep
on now, holiday

or no, my whole
morning messed up
by road-kill, wannabe

Presidents, street
bombs, cyberspace,
Bosnia, and what's to

become of the former
United States, an
America only once

divisible. Half-
blinded by freeflow
tears and new sun,

I find myself
still touched by
the woman talking

with sheep. I try
to figure what they
say to each other;

and when, if spring
happens, the new
lambs will come.

from *American Poetry Review*

Sea of Faith

◇   ◇   ◇

Once when I was teaching "Dover Beach"
to a class of freshmen, a young woman
raised her hand and said, "I'm confused
about this 'Sea of Faith.' " "Well," I said,
"let's talk about it. We probably need
to talk a bit about figurative language.
What confuses you about it?"
"I mean, is it a real sea?" she asked.
"You mean, is it a real body of water
that you could point to on a map
or visit on a vacation?"
"Yes," she said. "Is it a *real* sea?"
Oh Christ, I thought, is this where we are?
Next year I'll be teaching them the alphabet
and how to sound words out.
I'll have to teach them geography, apparently,
before we can move on to poetry.
I'll have to teach them history, too—
a few weeks on the Dark Ages might be instructive.
"Yes," I wanted to say, "it is.
It is a real sea. In fact it flows
right into the Sea of Ignorance
IN WHICH YOU ARE DROWNING.
Let me throw you a Rope of Salvation
before the Sharks of Desire gobble you up.
Let me hoist you back up onto this Ship of Fools
so that we might continue our search
for the Fountain of Youth. Here, take a drink
of this. It's fresh from the River of Forgetfulness."

But of course I didn't say any of that.
I tried to explain in such a way
as to protect her from humiliation,
tried to explain that poets
often speak of things that don't exist.
It was only much later that I wished
I could have answered differently,
only after I'd betrayed myself
and been betrayed that I wished
it was true, wished there really was a Sea of Faith
that you could wade out into,
dive under its blue and magic waters,
hold your breath, swim like a fish
down to the bottom, and then emerge again
able to believe in everything, faithful
and unafraid to ask even the simplest of questions,
happy to have them simply answered.

from *The Southern Review*

Because I Am

◇   ◇   ◇

For Sidney Bechet, 1897–1959

Because I am a memorious old man
I've been asked to write about you, Papa Sidney,
Improvising in standard meter on a well-known
Motif, as you did all those nights in Paris
And the world. I remember once in Chicago
On the Near North where you were playing with
A white band, how you became disgusted
And got up and sat in front next to the bandstand
And ordered four ponies of brandy; and then
You drank them one by one, and threw the empty
Glasses at the trumpet-player. Everyone laughed,
Of course, but you were dead serious—sitting there
With your fuzzy white head in your rumpled navy
Serge. When you lifted that brass soprano to your
Lips and blew, you were superb, the best of all,
The first and best, an *Iliad* to my ears.
And always your proper creole name was mis-
Pronounced. Now you are lost in the bad shadows
Of time past; you are a dark man in the darkness,
Who knew us all in music. Out of the future
I hear ten thousand saxophones mumbling
In your riffs and textures, Papa Sidney. And when
I stand up trembling in darkness to recite
I see sparkling glass ponies come sailing at me
Out of the reaches of the impermeable night.

from *Seneca Review*

the mississippi river empties into the gulf

◇   ◇   ◇

and the gulf enters the sea and so forth,
none of them emptying anything,
all of them carrying yesterday
forever on their white tipped backs,
all of them dragging forward tomorrow.
it is the great circulation
of the earth's body, like the blood
of the gods, this river in which the past
is always flowing. every water
is the same water coming round.
everyday someone is standing on the edge
of this river staring into time,
whispering mistakenly;
only here. only now.

from *River City*

Dharma

◊　◊　◊

The way the dog trots out the front door
every morning
without a hat or an umbrella,
without any money
or the keys to her dog house
never fails to fill the saucer of my heart
with milky admiration.

Who provides a finer example
of a life without encumbrance?
Thoreau in his curtainless hut
with a single plate, a single spoon?
Gandhi with his staff and his holy diapers?

Off she goes into the material world
with nothing but her brown coat
and her modest blue collar,
following only her wet nose,
the twin portals of her steady breathing,
followed only by the plume of her tail.

If only she did not shove the cat aside
every morning
and eat all his food
what a model of self-containment she would be,
what a paragon of earthly detachment.
If only she were not so eager

for a rub behind the ears,
so acrobatic in her welcomes,
if only I were not her god.

from *Poetry*

Mitch

◊   ◊   ◊

Mitch was a classmate
later married extraordinary poet
and so our families were friends
when we were all young
and lived in New York, New Hampshire, France.

He had eyes with whites
above eyeballs looked out
over lids in droll surmise—
"gone under earth's lid" was Pound's phrase,
cancered stomach?

A whispered information over phone,
two friends the past week . . . ,
the one, she says, an eccentric dear woman,
conflicted with son?
Convicted with ground

tossed in, one supposes,
more dead than alive.
Life's done all it could
for all of them.
Time to be gone?

Not since 1944–45
have I felt so dumbly, utterly,
in the wrong place at
entirely the wrong time,
caught then in that merciless war,

now trapped here, old, on a blossoming earth,
nose filled with burgeoning odors,
wind a caress, sound blurred reassurance,
echo of others, the lovely compacting
human warmths, the eye closing upon you,

seeing eye, sight's companion, dark or light,
makes out of its lonely distortions
it's you again, coming closer, feel
weight in the bed beside me,
close to my bones.

They told me it would be
like this but who could
believe it, not to leave, not to
go away? "I'll hate to
leave this earthly paradise . . ."

There's no time like the present,
no time in the present. Now it floats, goes out like a boat
upon the sea. Can't we see,
can't we now be company
to that one of us

has to go? *Hold my hand, dear.*
I should have hugged him,
taken him up, held him,
in my arms. I should
have let him know I was here.

Is it my turn now,
who's to say or wants to?
You're not sick, there are
certainly those older.
Your time will come.

In God's hands it's cold.
In the universe it's an empty, echoing silence.
Only us to make sounds,
but I made none.
I sat there like a stone.

from *Solo*

Betrayal

◇   ◇   ◇

In her fantasies about other men, as she grew older, about men other than her husband, she no longer dreamed of sexual intimacy, as she once had, perhaps for revenge, when she was angry, perhaps out of loneliness, when he was angry, but only about an affection and a profound sort of understanding, a holding of hands and a gazing into eyes, often in a public place like a café. She did not know if this change came out of respect for her husband, for she did truly respect him, or out of plain weariness, at the end of the day, or out of a sense of what activity she could expect from herself, even in a fantasy, now that she was a certain age. And when she was particularly tired, she couldn't even manage the affection and the profound understanding, but only the mildest sort of companionship, such as being in the same room alone together, sitting in chairs. And it happened that as she grew older still, and more tired, and then still older, and still more tired, another change occurred and she found that even the mildest sort of companionship, alone together, was now too vigorous to sustain, and her fantasies were limited to a calm sort of friendliness among other friends, the sort she really could have had with any man, with a clear conscience, and did in fact have with many, who were friends of her husband's too, or not, a friendliness that gave her comfort and strength, at night, when the friendships in her waking life were not enough, or had not been enough by the end of the day. And so these fantasies came to be indistinguishable from the reality of her waking life, and should not have been any sort of betrayal at all. Yet because they were fantasies she had alone, at night, they continued to feel like some sort of betrayal, and perhaps, because approached in this spirit of betrayal, as perhaps they had to be, any comfort and strength, continued to be, in fact, a sort of betrayal.

from *Hambone*

Taproot

◇   ◇   ◇

Stooping to pull up a weed,
I think of my father
who made of weeding an art.

After work, he'd take a bucket
and his weeder from the toolshed
and clear an area of a yard he knew

would never look manicured,
whose quality would, at best,
be like something homemade.

He'd set the bucket upside down
and sit on it. Plotting a route
he'd shift the bucket, a move

so deft you might think he was just
leaning out to extend his reach.
He knew exactly where and what angle

to drive the weeder down,
north and south of the weed,
without severing its taproot.

When my father worked like this,
making small mounds he'd later
gather up in his bucket,

the dog would sniff at his bare feet
then lie down in the shade his body made.
Grounded there, he was most himself,

his hunger for perfection and control
giving way, finally, to the work itself.
It was easy to love him then.

from *Crab Orchard Review*

Pasternak

◇   ◇   ◇

What century have we got out there, my dears?
—BORIS PASTERNAK

This was the life, to live in Russia
at the end of Russia and write about its history
as if it were poetry, while one beloved or the other
lay asleep nearby, dreaming of him writing nearby
in a high ceilinged room with the vista
of snow-covered mountains, forests and fields.
More ice than glass in the window frames.
A red coal in the samovar.
Outside, in the distance, the endless rain
of shells and sough of trains behind the hills.
The old world falling to its knees like an elephant.

This was the life, to live at Peredelkino
like a prophet in his own land and dream.
"What I have lost is much too great for a single man,"
he writes in the snow with the tip of his cane.
The shelling has stopped and the world has changed.
The wind picks up and blows the words away.
He writes for the eyes who follow him,
"Nothing is lost in the other world."
This dark December day inspires him to write
the plainest things in the snow, then walk away.

from *New England Review*

Madam's Heart

◇　◇　◇

She had fallen in love with her doctor's stethoscope; the way it listened to her heart . . .

The doctor said, would you like to honeymoon with my telescope? You should see how it extends itself and looks into the night for the heavenly body.

Oh, but your microscope is so nearsighted . . .

Then how about my periscope? It rises out of the mattress with a cunning eye for backdoors.

That's even more disgusting than that kaleidoscope; the way it fixes me with its fractured cyclops eye.

Finally the doctor holds up his stethoscope and wiggles it at her and asks, is madam ready?

Oh, yes, she sighed . . .

from *The Prose Poem*

A Buddha
in the Woodpile

◊ ◊ ◊

If there had been only
one Buddhist in the woodpile
in Waco Texas
to teach us how to sit still
one saffron Buddhist in the back rooms
just one Tibetan lama
just one Taoist
just one Thomas Merton Trappist
just one saint in the wilderness
of Waco USA
If there had been only one
calm little Gandhi
in a white sheet or suit
one not-so-silent partner
who at the last moment shouted *Wait*
If there had been just one
majority of one
in the lotus position
in the inner sanctum
who bowed his shaved head to the
Chief of All Police
and raised his hands in a mudra
and chanted the Great Paramita Sutra
the Diamond Sutra
the Lotus Sutra
If there had somehow been

just one Gandhian spinner
with Brian Willson at the gates of the White House
at the Gates of Eden
then it wouldn't have been
Vietnam once again
and its "One two three four
What're we waitin' for?"
if one single ray of the light
of the Dalai Lama
when he visited this land
had penetrated somehow
the Land of the Brave
where the lion never
lies down with the lamb—
But not a glimmer got through
The Security screened it out
screened out the Buddha
and his not-so-crazy wisdom
If only in the land of Sam Houston
if only in the land of the Alamo
if only in Wacoland USA
if only in Reno
if only on CNN CBS NBC
one had comprehended
one single syllable
of the Gautama Buddha
of the young Siddhartha
one single whisper of
Gandhi's spinning wheel
one lost syllable
of Martin Luther King
or of the Early Christians
or of Mother Teresa
or Thoreau or Whitman or Allen Ginsberg
or of the millions in America tuned to *them*
If the inner ears of the inner sanctums
had only been half open
to any vibrations except
those of the national security state
and had only been attuned

to the sound of one hand clapping
and not one hand punching
Then that sick cult and its children
might still be breathing
the free American air
of the First Amendment

from *Blasts!*

My Father's Fields

◇　◇　◇

September 1918

They looked like blackbirds, my father said,
that first burst of shrapnel,
spiraling up in autumn flight,
and at first that's what he thought they were,
their glossy wings catching the sun
as they wheeled in the morning sky.

There was that moment of beauty,
the glint of it,
in that first day on the Meuse-Argonne
before the earth came off its perch,
as if they had offended it somehow,
or that's the thought he had, he said,
the earth rising up over every stored transgression,
and what had they done to bring this on?

Later it was all the dead horses,
the field before the river strewn with horses,
and his friend, Carl Johnson,
sleeping off the numbness of battle,
at peace almost,
but for the way his leg wrapped up behind him,
and the too-wide smile
of the bloody mouth across his neck,
Carl playing dead among the horses; he thought
of Carl with his Belgians at the county fair.

90,000 horses moving up the roads at night.
He'd never imagined so many horses
in the history of the world,
or so many men in their silent march,
imagining no longer, the September morning
as they looked out on the manicured stubble
of the burnt-gold fields
and the still green trees in the haze
along the river.

These few things he noted in his journal,
though he spoke to me only of the horses,
the things people said, and the newly shorn fields.

The trees along the river are what I see
when I think my father's thoughts,
not the fiery sky, the tangled wire,
the splintered forest or all the dead horses,
but those fields shorn of wheat,
as his father's fields would be in September.

from *Poetry*

Vita Nova

◊　◊　◊

You saved me, you should remember me.

The spring of the year; young men buying tickets for the ferry boats.
Laughter, because the air is full of apple blossoms.

When I woke up, I realized I was capable of the same feeling.

I remember sounds like that from my childhood,
laughter for no cause, simply because the world is beautiful,
something like that.

Lugano. Tables under the apple trees.
Deckhands raising and lowering the colored flags.
And by the lake's edge, a young man throws his hat into the water;
perhaps his sweetheart has accepted him.

Crucial
sounds or gestures like
a track laid down before the larger themes

and then unused, buried.

Islands in the distance. My mother
holding out a plate of little cakes—

as far as I remember, changed
in no detail, the moment
vivid, intact, having never been
exposed to light, so that I woke elated, at my age
hungry for life, utterly confident—

By the tables, patches of new grass, the pale green
pierced into the dark existing ground.

Surely spring has been returned to me, this time
not as a lover but a messenger of death, yet
it is still spring, it is still meant tenderly.

from *The New Yorker*

Breastbone

◇   ◇   ◇

*In Mexico, a young boy is bitten by a snake and lies
paralyzed for months. His grandfather, a shaman, predicts
that if he lives he will become a great leader.*

He lives and becomes Llaga, the blind man
who sees through his nipples.
He wears no shirt, his bare chest adorned
with beads from broken beer bottles.
He has polished them, hung them around his neck,
brown glass reflecting what he can't see,
hiding him from the people who trust him for advice.

His nipples are dark and wrinkled.
They never rise or harden.
They must stay close to his heart,
so he can remind those around him
his eyes were the nests of the rattler that bit him,
the oval entrances to their dying town.
His chest is turning gray.
Thin hair on it surrounds his eyes.
When he bathes in the river,
he can see under the water.

No one in the town knows the name Llaga.
He tells no one, but the name is there.
It can be found in the thought that blinks
inside the first stranger to approach him.
Llaga does not reveal many things.
His drum is torn.

He can't be described without his white hair
woven around his neck, hanging
between his shoulder blades like the rope
the strangers tried to hang him with,
years ago, before he discovered
he could see through his nipples.

The young boy survived.
He could see.
He opened his eyes.
The fresh strips of snake meat hung,
dripping a white liquid on the pole.
Years had not passed.
It was only a moment
in the life of the fang.

from *The Bitter Oleander*

The Last Election

◇　◇　◇

Suppose there are no returns,
and the candidates, one
by one, drop off in the polls,
as the voters turn away,
each to his inner persuasion.

The frontrunners, the dark horses,
begin to look elsewhere,
and even the President admits
he has nothing new to say;
it is best to be silent now.

No more conventions, no donors,
no more hats in the ring;
no ghost-written speeches,
no promises we always knew
were never meant to be kept.

And something like the truth,
or what we knew by that name—
that for which no corporate
sponsor was ever offered—
takes hold in the public mind.

Each subdued and thoughtful
citizen closes his door, turns
off the news. He opens a book,
speaks quietly to his children,
begins to live once more.

from *Many Mountains Moving*

Smile

◇　◇　◇

She was twenty-five when they settled in our town.
When they moved from the city into their colonial
they unpacked wedding china and silver from boxes
labeled *Tiffany, Bergdorf Goodman,* and *K-Mart.*
Both men and women leaned like peonies
toward the luster and power of her unlimited
determining smile. They brought with them a small son
and she bore two daughters in five years.
She dressed her children in primary colors
so that they resembled child models in a catalog,
yet they played with such charm they made childhood
seem happy. Her handsome husband adored her.
Many remembered the photograph in the *Courier*
when they first came to town: She sits upright,
baby on her lap and husband smiling behind her.
Even the baby smiles, but it is her mouth
that flashes outward from the gray of newsprint.
When new photographs appeared, over the years
of dances and fund drives, they repeated
the same smile inhabiting an aging face.
She confessed to a lover how she summoned
her generous smile for the camera: As she gazed
into the lens she thought *prick asshole cunt.*

　　　We loved her and nothing diminished our love.
When they arrived they joined the Purple Hills Club,
which provided them a set. Many husbands
from the Club followed her the way kindergartners
follow their teachers, but even the plainest wives
never disliked her for long. When a friend

turned cold, she telephoned her and suggested
lunch at the Club. After an engaging conversation,
with many smiles, the friend was convinced
of warmth, fidelity, good faith, and disinterest.

She played an energetic game of tennis,
mostly doubles on Tuesday and Thursday afternoons
with her seven closest friends. She was elected
president of the Purple Hills Garden Club.
Mornings before his dayschool she drove her son
to hockey practice, afternoons her daughters
to ballet. For their birthdays she hired a team
of puppeteers or a magician. With contract bridge
partners from the Club, she and her husband
went to numerous cocktail and dinner parties
on Friday and Saturday evenings, so many
that they found it difficult to reciprocate.
In spring and autumn, they mounted cocktail
parties employing a jazz trio they imported
from the city. Six times a year, she prepared
dinner for twelve. She cooked for two days
and hired students to help with the serving.

In their first decade here, Purple Hills Club
people danced together at their weekend parties.
If there was a husband for whom she smiled least,
her friends speculated that he was the moment's
favorite. Sundays she and her husband played
mixed doubles with three other couples, then
concluded the busy weekend by meeting for potluck
at somebody's house. It was her crab bisque
that we praised the most. When we complimented
her cooking—or her tennis or her bridge—
we received the smile we looked for. Monday
mornings her husband fixed her French toast
and coffee in bed and delivered the children
to their schools. Tuesdays from 10:30
until lunchtime she read aloud to a blind widow
from John Ruskin's *Fors Clavigera*. Her hair
appointment was for three p.m. on Fridays.

As they advanced into their late forties,
Purple Hills couples went to fewer cocktail

parties and played less tennis. Some died.
Some stopped drinking. Her smile remained
all the more bright for the lines on her face.
One child gave them problems; it seemed unfair
for trouble to visit her house. Her husband's
sideburns went gray; her own hair turned auburn
and no one was unkind. For five years running
she was first runner-up in Senior Singles; she
might have won, people thought, if she had tried.

    After her children were grown, she returned
to the State University to pick up an M.A.
in the History of Art, writing on a graphic
designer from the *belle époque*. When a young man
whom she met in the Department—teaching fellow
and Ph.D. candidate—boarded with them, taking
a child's room, it was clear that her growing old
was ruinous. It was *after* the young man died,
as the malicious rumors neglected to mention,
that someone broke into their house in their absence,
ripping upholstery and the Picasso print, carving
prick asshole cunt into the bedroom wallpaper.
For two weeks she remained housebound, then returned
smiling, despite the gossip. Some years later,
in her illness, she was a beautiful invalid.
If anything her smile remained set in its place
for a moment longer. When she lost flesh
her cheekbones stood out; the whole town spoke
of her courage and cheer. Everyone offered to help.
The child who had become a problem returned
to her bedside at the end, which made her smile.

    All this happened long ago. She lies under
ground in a box perfect with darkness, her flesh
fallen away except for corrupted shreds on her skull
where the mortician fashioned a replica of her smile.
Each of her aging grandchildren displays
her photograph on a staircase wall of family
photographs. Visitors take notice of her smile.

from *The Yale Review*

September

◇   ◇   ◇

Tonight there must be people who are getting what they want.
I let my oars fall into the water.
Good for them. Good for them, getting what they want.

The night is so still that I forget to breathe.
The dark air is getting colder. Birds are leaving.

Tonight there are people getting just what they need.

The air is so still that it seems to stop my heart.
I remember you in a black and white photograph
taken this time of some year. You were leaning against
a half-shed tree, standing in the leaves the tree had lost.

When I finally exhale it takes forever to be over.

Tonight, there are people who are so happy,
that they have forgotten to worry about tomorrow.

Somewhere, people have entirely forgotten about tomorrow.
My hand trails in the water.
I should not have dropped those oars. Such a soft wind.

from *The Antioch Review*

What Would Freud Say?

◇ ◇ ◇

Wasn't on purpose that I drilled
through my finger or the nurse
laughed. She apologized
three times and gave me a shot
of something that was a lusher
apology. The person
who drove me home
said my smile was a smeared
totem that followed
his body that night as it arced
over a cliff in a dream.
He's always flying
in his dreams and lands
on cruise ships or hovers
over Atlanta with an erection.
He put me to bed and the drugs
wore off and I woke
to cannibals at my extremities.
I woke with a sense
of what nails in the palms
might do to a spirit
temporarily confined to flesh.
That too was an accident
if you believe Judas
merely wanted to be loved.
To be loved by God,
Urban the 8th
had heads cut off
that were inadequately

bowed by dogma. To be loved
by Blondie, Dagwood
gets nothing right
except the hallucinogenic
architecture of sandwiches.
He would have drilled
through a finger too
while making a case for books
on home repair and health.
Drilling through my finger's
not the dumbest thing
I've done. Second place
was approaching
a frozen gas-cap with lighter
in hand while thinking
heat melts ice and not
explosion kills asshole. First
place was passing
through a bedroom door
and removing silk that did not
belong to my wife.
Making a bookcase is not
the extent of my apology.
I've also been beaten up
in a bar for saying huevos
rancheros in a way
insulting to the patrons'
ethnicity. I've also lost
my job because lying
face down on the couch
didn't jibe with my employer's
definition of home
office. I wanted her to come
through the door on Sunday
and see the bookcase
she'd asked me to build
for a year and be impressed
that it didn't lean
or wobble even though
I've only leaned and often

wobbled. Now it's half
done but certainly
a better gift with its map
of my unfaithful blood.

from *Cream City Review*

The Envoy

◊   ◊   ◊

One day in that room, a small rat.
Two days later, a snake.

Who, seeing me enter,
whipped the long stripe of his
body under the bed,
then curled like a docile house-pet.

I don't know how either came or left.
Later, the flashlight found nothing.

For a year I watched
as something—terror? happiness? grief?—
entered and then left my body.

Not knowing how it came in,
Not knowing how it went out.

It hung where words could not reach it.
It slept where light could not go.
Its scent was neither snake nor rat,
neither sensualist nor ascetic.

There are openings in our lives
of which we know nothing.

Through them
the belled herds travel at will,
long-legged and thirsty, covered with foreign dust.

from *Blue Sofa*

Lawrence

◇ ◇ ◇

On two occasions in the past twelve months
I have failed, when someone at a party
spoke of him with a dismissive scorn,
to stand up for D. H. Lawrence,

a man who burned like an acetylene torch
from one end to the other of his life.
These individuals, whose relationship to literature
is approximately that of a tree shredder

to stands of old-growth forest,
these people leaned back in their chairs,
bellies full of dry white wine and the ovum of some foreign fish,
and casually dropped his name

the way pygmies with their little poison spears
strut around the carcass of a fallen elephant.
"O Elephant," they say,
"you are not so big and brave today!"

It's a bad day when people speak of their superiors
with a contempt they haven't earned,
and it's a sorry thing when certain other people

don't defend the great dead ones
who have opened up the world before them.
And though, in the catalogue of my betrayals,
this is a fairly minor entry,

I resolve, if the occasion should recur,
to uncheck my tongue and say; "I love the spectacle
of maggots condescending to a corpse,"
or, "You should be so lucky in your brainy, bloodless life

as to deserve to lift
just one of D. H. Lawrence's urine samples
to your arid psychobiographic
theory-tainted lips."

Or maybe I'll just take the shortcut
between the spirit and the flesh,
and punch someone in the face,
because human beings haven't come that far

in their effort to subdue the body,
and we still walk around like zombies
in our dying, burning world,
able to do little more

than fight, and fuck, and crow,
something Lawrence wrote about
in such a manner
as to make us seem magnificent.

from *Ploughshares*

Beach Whispers

◇   ◇   ◇

In the night wind astir
The pale dune grasses sing
"We are what we always whirr,
Food for ruminant thought,"
Soft, neither out of tune
Nor in it as their commotion
Mingles with the hiss
Of water falling all over
Itself to claim the sand.
Ears open and eyes shut
We barely understand
What they could be said to say
About the neap and spring
Of tides and even more
About how to uncover
The orders of all this:
The crown of the bright moon,
The fiefdom of the ocean,
The serfdom of the shore,
(Such dark politics) and,
Nightly feigning his role
Of deus absconditus, sole
Absentee landlord of all,
Some otherwhere the sun
Reigns from his distant hall.

from *The New Yorker*

Man Script

◇   ◇   ◇

Membrane is parchment,
or so the words unite in seed
of Middle English earth. Once,
in experiment, a bunch of us
wrote lines of poetry

in Magik Marker on a naked
man lying face down on some
coats at The Drawing Center.
Not quite erotic like *The Pillow
Book* would be, but I did think

of this man and his woman
later sweating our words onto
their sheets before enough showers
could soap us censored. Not
a dead sheep's skin with gold

leaf but yet an illuminated
text, or breathing parchment.
Forget where we started, this
evening of written exquisite corpse
took a turn past the original 1920s

drawings on the gallery walls.
Lines disembodied and suggestive,
these exercises are like Mad
Libs, only they bring us back to
lyric, the unimaginable body

made beautiful despite its
frog legs and women's hands. Our
bearded gentleman deferred to
his girlfriend when his name was
drawn, but she mocked, it's up

to you. Lights dimmed to a
filament darkness or protective
tissue, he stripped, swiftly, with
effortless moves, as if his clothes
and modesty were just taped on.

None of us budged, at first,
suddenly thoughtful of home, or
dinner, but then advanced as
a flock of shy, dumb sheep with
indelible ink thoughts. I put my

small nephew's fear of fire
in the trees below the man's left
shoulder blade. No one wrote on his
pale ass. We were told by our leader
to read from him all at once,

cancelling all effort to create
a body of work. He was just a color
scrawl and we, as indistinct
in voice as a restaurant crowd.
I'm glad my coat was not beneath

his strange penis, nor my skin
tickled by the tentative,
slimy strokes of soaked felt.
Eros and the Muses had skipped out
early, and when I reached the

street, I saw the night
had a brilliancy like the first
time I drank too much tequila
and turned my head—all vivid
and a little bit shiny.

from *Literal Latté*

DAVID IGNATOW

The Story of Progress

◇   ◇   ◇

The apple I held and bit into was for me. The friend who spoke to me was for me. My father and mother were for me. The little girl with brown hair and brown eyes who looked and smiled shyly and ran away was for me, although I never dared follow her because I feared she would not understand that she was for me alone.

The bed I slept in was for me. The clothes I wore were for me. The kindness I showed a dead bird one winter by placing it in my warm pocket was for me. The time I went to the rescue of my sister from a bully was to prove myself, for me. The music on the radio, the books I was beginning to read, all were for me.

I had hold of a good thing, me, and I was going to give of my contentment to others, for me, and when I gave, it was taken with a smile that I recognized as mine, when I would be given. I had found that for me was everybody's way, and I became anxious and uncertain. I held back a bit when I exchanged post card pictures of baseball players, with a close look at what I was getting in return to make sure I was getting what I could like, and when my parents bought me a new pair of gloves after I had lost the first pair I was sure that for me was not as pure in feeling as the first time, because I was very sorry that my parents had to spend an extra dollar to replace my lost gloves, and so when I looked up at the night stars, for me remained silent, and when my grandmother died, for me became a little boy sent on an errand of candles to place at the foot and head of her coffin.

from *Verse*

The Circle Theatre

◇　◇　◇

They would go around noon, separated by a minute
or two, both of them working at the Academy then.
He wore sports jackets. She wore dresses and high
heels. They crossed Pennsylvania at 21ˢᵗ, entered
a lobby, rode up six flights. They were above
the Circle Theatre, all that spring showing
De Sica's *The Garden of the Finzi-Continis.*
Their friend Joseph rented this room for meditation:
A mattress, his blue satsang cushion mid-floor,
an incense boat, a small brass gong, a postcard
photo of his maharishi. The parquet was old,
scrubbed colorless. Through the slats at the
window—The White House, and beyond,
the Washington Monument, the Capitol dome.
The city abuzz with the word *impeachment,*
Nixon was that madman who schemed
five blocks east of them. In that room he
first entered her from behind. She was staring
across the floor at the blue cushion, the ridge
of his teeth scuffing the rim of her left ear,
his words lost, though of love. While they
were wholly transfixed by sensation in that lost
extravagant way, a bright wheat-colored light
unfolded across the walls and floor. The presence
Joseph had called so often to that place, must approve
of their passion; this new light, a sign of blessing.

This was the meaning settled on as they dressed.
At their peak, cherry and crabapple wavered above
beds of tulips, cast a delicate brume over the city.

from *Alkali Flats*

Last Will and Testament

◊　◊　◊

At the lowest points, he went
into a restaurant (maybe three a night)
and took a menu to study;

pocketed half a dozen cubes
of sugar, drank cold good water, ate,
if there was one, a roll,

Found the menu flat
and unprofitable, left, between
busboy and waiter.

Repetition impossible;
but lots of restaurants in winter
Manhattan.

The odd reading, or loan, or donkeywork
helped. Writing, he chose and chose.
He wrote good poetry.

He wrote honed out-of-season
lyrics. Some got printed
and achieved a mini-reputation.

He wrote lines better than good
and one monosyllabic
indestructible phrase

that can't wear or fade or chip.
I can't remember the title
of the poem it came from.

Six monosyllables. Enough.
My copy slipped away;
it was a paperback

of which I had five copies.
They all went somewhere before,
or after, he died.

He gave a small reading
in a formal house:
receptive people.

Too long, after the reading,
he said and drank too much. The hostess
rose to everything

until he went to bed and put
his shoes outside the door.
They did get shined.

I can't remember what went—heart
or liver, or at what age.
He had thick eyelashes

(behind glasses) and a trustworthy
wit. But the phrase, the five
placed words, visit

my moon's glimpses, and certain
silences. I don't know how many
possess them.

He wrote the phrase that said
. . . The last great look of loss . . . "The last
great
look
of
loss."

from *Potomac Review*

Two
Prose Poems

◇   ◇   ◇

THE FISHING LURE

I've spent a great deal of my life fretting over things that most people wouldn't waste their time on. Trying to explain something I haven't a clue about. It's given me that worried look, that wide-eyed, staring look. The look that wild animals sometimes have, deer for instance, trying to make sense of the situation: "What *is* that?" Motionless, trans-fixed. The same look that's on the face of the fishing lure. Stupidity? Terror? What is the right bait for these conditions? High cirrus clouds, cold front moving in. It's all a trick anyway. What is this thing supposed to be? A minnow? A bug? Gaudy paint and hooks all over. It's like bleached blond hair and bright red lipstick. Nobody *really* believes it. There isn't a way in the world I'd bite on that thing. But I might swim in just a little closer.

THE LIFE OF THE POET

I once believed that behind all the things I did, or more often, failed to do, there was a great moral purpose, or at least some coherent princi-ple, a *raison d'être*. If there is such a principle it has never become quite clear to me. Instead, over the years, I have managed to take a random selection of bad habits and herd them together into a life. Also, in order to disguise my absolute laziness I have mastered the age-old art of appearing to be productive when, actually, *this* is the only thing I'm doing. (Republicans suspected as much all along.) Someone comes up to my desk and I get busy scribbling, totally preoccupied. "What? Oh, I'm sorry. . . ."In my haste to appear industrious I find I have written ". . . and herd them together into a *wife.*"

from *Rosebud*

The Patient

◇   ◇   ◇

At the end we prayed for death,
even phoned funeral homes
from his room for the best

cremation deal. But back
when he was tall, he once put
my ailing cat to sleep,

or helped the vet and me
hold it flat to the table
while we felt all muscles

tighten for escape
then freeze that way. Later
in my father's truck,

I held the heavy shoebox on my lap.
He said, I ever git like that
you do the same. I remember the slight

weight of my ten-year-old head
nodding without a pause. We peeled
from the gravel lot onto the rain-

blurred road. What did I know
of patience then? Or my dad
for that matter, shifting gears.

Each white second was knit
into a sheet that settled over his features
like a snowfield. Forgive me,

Father, this penitent face.
I was the patient one.
I got what I wanted.

from *Poetry*

A Curse on a Thief

◇   ◇   ◇

Paul Dempster had a handsome tackle box
In which he'd stored up gems for many years:
Hooks marvelously sharp, ingenious lures
Jointed to look alive. He went to Fox

Lake, placed it on his dock, went in and poured
Himself a frosty Coors, returned to find
Some craven sneak had stolen in behind
His back and crooked his entire treasure horde.

Bad cess upon the bastard! May the bass
He catches with Paul Dempster's pilfered gear
Jump from his creel, make haste for his bare rear,
And, fins outthrust, slide up his underpass.

May each ill-gotten catfish in his pan
Sizzle his lips and peel away the skin.
May every perch his pilfered lines reel in
Oblige him to spend decades on the can.

May he be made to munch a pickerel raw,
Its steely eyes fixed on him as he chews,
Choking on every bite, while metal screws
Inexorably lock his lower jaw,

And having eaten, may he be transformed
Into a trout himself, with gills and scales,
A stupid gasper that a hook impales.
In Hell's hot griddle may he be well warmed

And served with shots of lava-on-the-rocks
To shrieking imps indifferent to his moans
Who'll rend his skin and pick apart his bones,
Poor fish who hooked Paul Dempster's tackle box.

from *Harvard Review*

Why Regret?

◇　◇　◇

Didn't you like the way the ants help
the peony globes open by eating off the glue?
Weren't you cheered to see the ironworkers
sitting on an I-beam dangling from a cable,
in a row, like starlings, eating lunch, maybe
baloney on white with fluorescent mustard?
Wasn't it a revelation to waggle from the estuary
all the way up the river, the pirle,
the kill, the run, the brook, the beck,
the sike gone dry, to the shock of a spring?
Didn't you almost shiver, hearing the book lice
clicking their sexual syncopation inside the old
Webster's *New International*—perhaps having just
eaten out of it *izle, xyster* and *thalassacon?*
What did you imagine lay in store anyway
at the end of a world whose sub-substance is
ooze, gleet, birdlime, slime, mucus, muck?
Don't worry about becoming emaciated—think of the wren
and how little flesh is needed to make a song.
Didn't it seem somehow familiar when the nymph
split open and the mayfly struggled free
and flew and perched and then its own back split open
and the imago, the true adult, somersaulted
out backwards and took flight
toward the swarm, mouth-parts vestigial,
alimentary canal unfit to digest food,
a day or hour left to find the desired one?
Or when Casanova threw the linguine in squid ink
out the window, telling his startled companion,

"The perfected lover does not eat."
As a child didn't you find it calming to think
of the pinworms as some kind of tiny batons
giving cadence to the squeezes and releases
around the downward march of debris?
Didn't you once glimpse what seemed your
own inner blazonry in the monarchs, wobbling
and gliding, in desire, in the middle air?
Weren't you reassured at the thought that these flimsy,
hinged beings might navigate their way to Mexico
by the flair of the dead bodies of ancestors
who fell in the same migration a year ago?
Isn't it worth missing whatever joy
you might have dreamed, to wake in the night and find
you and your beloved are holding hands in your sleep?

from *The New Yorker*

The Erotic Philosophers

◇　◇　◇

It's a spring morning; sun pours in the window
As I sit here drinking coffee, reading Augustine.
And finding him, as always, newly minted
From when I first encountered him in school.
Today I'm overcome with astonishment
At the way we girls denied all that was mean
In those revered philosophers we studied;
Who found us loathsome, loathsomely seductive;
Irrelevant at best to noble discourse
Among the sex, the only sex that counted.
Wounded, we pretended not to mind it
And wore tight sweaters to tease our shy professor.

We sat in autumn sunshine "as the clouds arose
From slimy desires of the flesh, and from
Youth's seething spring." Thank you, Augustine.
Attempting to seem blasé, our cheeks on fire
It didn't occur to us to rush from the room
Instead, we brushed aside "the briars of unclean desire"
And struggled on through mires of misogyny
Till we arrived at Kierkegaard, and began to see
That though Saint A. and Søren had much in common
Including fear and trembling before women,
The Saint scared himself, while Søren was scared of *us*.
Had we, poor girls, been flattered by their thralldom?

Yes, it was always us, the rejected feminine
From whom temptation came. It was our flesh
With its deadly sweetness that led them on.

Yet how could we not treasure Augustine,
"stuck fast in the birdlime of pleasure"?
That roomful of adolescent poets manqué
Assuaged, bemused by music, let the meaning go.
Swept by those psalmic cadences, we were seduced!
Some of us tried for awhile to be well-trained souls
And pious seekers, enmeshed in the Saint's dialectic:
Responsible for our actions, yet utterly helpless.
A sensible girl would have barked like a dog before God.

We students, children still, were shocked to learn
The children these men desired were younger than we!
Augustine fancied a girl two years below
The age of consent; was she then eight or ten?
Søren, like Poe, eyed his girl before she was sixteen.
To impose his will on a malleable child, when
She was not equipped to withstand or understand him.
Ah, the Pygmalion instinct! Mold the clay!
Create the compliant doll that can only obey,
Expecting to be abandoned, minute by minute.
It was then I abandoned philosophy,
A minor loss, although I majored in it.

But we were a group of sunny innocents.
I don't believe we knew what evil meant.
Now I live with a well-trained soul who deals with evil
Including error, material or spiritual,
Easily, like changing a lock on the kitchen door.
He prays at set times and in chosen places
(at meals, in church), while I
Pray without thinking how or when to pray,
In a low mumble, several times a day,
Like running a continuous low fever;
The sexual impulse for the most part being over.
Believing I believe. Not banking on it ever.

It's afternoon. I sit here drinking kir
And reading Kierkegaard: "All sin begins with fear."
(True. We lie first from terror of our parents.)
In, I believe, an oblique crack at Augustine,

Søren said by denying the erotic
It was brought to the attention of the world.
The rainbow curtain rises on the sensual:
Christians must admit it before they can deny it.
He reflected on his father's fierce repression
Of the sexual, which had bent him out of shape:
Yet he had to pay obeisance to that power:
He chose his father when he broke with his Regina.

Søren said by denying the erotic
It is brought to the attention of the world.
You must admit it before you can deny it.
So much for "Repetition"—another theory
Which some assume evolved from his belief
He could replay his courtship of Regina
With a happy ending. Meanwhile she'd wait for him,
Eternally faithful, eternally seventeen.
Instead, within two years, the bitch got married.
In truth, he couldn't wait till he got rid of her,
To create from recollection, not from living;
To use the material, not the material girl.

I sip my kir, thinking of *Either/Or,*
Especially *Either,* starring poor Elvira.
He must have seen *Giovanni* a score of times,
And Søren knew the score.
He took Regina to the opera only once,
And as soon as Mozart's overture was over,
Kierkegaard stood up and said, "Now we are leaving.
You have heard the best: the expectation of pleasure."
In his interminable aria on the subject
SK insisted the performance *was* the play.
Was the overture then the foreplay? Poor Regina
Should have known she'd be left waiting in the lurch.

Though he chose a disguise in which to rhapsodize
It was his voice too: Elvira's beauty
Would perish soon; the deflowered quickly fade:
A night-blooming cereus after Juan's one-night stand.
Søren, eyes clouded by romantic mist,

Portrayed Elvira always sweet sixteen.
SK's interpretation seems naive.
He didn't realize that innocent sopranos
Who are ready to sing Elvira, don't exist.
His diva may have had it off with Leporello
Just before curtain time, believing it freed her voice
(so backstage legend has it), and weakened his.

I saw La Stupenda sing Elvira once.
Her cloak was larger than an army tent.
Would Giovanni be engulfed when she inhaled?
Would the boards shiver when she stamped her foot?
Her voice of course was great. Innocent it was not.
Søren, long since, would have fallen in a faint.
When he, or his doppelgänger, wrote
That best-seller, "The Diary of a Seducer,"
He showed how little he knew of true Don Juans:
Those turgid letters, machinations and excursions,
Those tedious conversations with dull aunts,
Those convoluted efforts to get the girl!

Think of the worldly European readers
Who took Søren seriously, did not see
His was the cynicism of the timid virgin.
Once in my youth I knew a real Don Juan
Or he knew me. He didn't need to try,
The characteristic of a true seducer.
He seems vulnerable, shy; he hardly speaks.
Somehow you know he will never speak of you.
You trust him—and you thrust yourself at him.
He responds with an almost absent-minded grace.
Even before the consummation he's looking past you
For the next bright yearning pretty face.

Relieved at last of anxieties and tensions
When your terrible efforts to capture him are over,
You overflow with happy/unhappy languor.
But SK's alter ego believes the truly terrible
Is for you to be consoled by the love of another.
We women, deserted to a woman, have a duty

Rapidly to lose our looks, decline and die,
Our only chance of achieving romantic beauty.
So Augustine was sure, when Monica, his mother,
Made him put aside his nameless concubine
She'd get her to a nunnery, and pine.
He chose his mother when he broke with his beloved.

In Søren's long replay of his wrecked romance,
"Guilty/Not Guilty," he says he must tear himself away
From earthly love, and suffer to love God.
Augustine thought better: love, human therefore flawed,
Is the way to the love of God. To deny this truth
Is to be "left outside, breathing into the dust,
Filling the eyes with earth." We women,
Outside, breathing dust, are still the Other.
The evening sun goes down; time to fix dinner.
"You women have no major philosophers." We know.
But we remain philosophic, and say with the Saint,
"Let me enter my chamber and sing my songs of love."

from *The Yale Review*

1989

◇　◇　◇

Because AIDS was slaughtering people left and right,
　　I went to a lot of memorial services that year.
There were so many, I'd pencil them in between
　　a movie or a sale at Macy's. The other thing that
made them tolerable was the funny stories people
　　got up and told about the deceased: the time he
hurled a mushroom frittata across a crowded room,
　　those green huaraches he refused to throw away,
the joke about the flight attendant and the banana
　　that cracked him up every time.

But this funeral was for a blind friend of my wife's
　　who'd merely died. And the interesting thing
about it was the guide dogs; with all the harness
　　and the sniffing around, the vestibule of the church
looked like the starting line of the Iditarod. But
　　nobody got up to talk. We just sat there
and the pastor read the King James version. Then he
　　said someday we would see Robert and he us.

Throughout the service, the dogs slumped beside their
　　masters. But when the soloist stood and launched
into a screechy rendition of "Abide with Me," they sank
　　into the carpet. A few put their paws over their ears.
Someone whispered to one of the blind guys; he told
　　another, and the laughter started to spread. People
in the back looked around, startled and embarrassed,

until they spotted all those chunky Labradors
flattened out like animals in a cartoon about
steamrollers. Then they started, too.

That was more like it. That was what I was used to—
a roomful of people laughing and crying, taking off
their sunglasses to blot their inconsolable eyes.

from *Solo*

Scapegoat

◇　◇　◇

The alpha wolf chooses his mate
For life, & the other she-wolves
Stare at the ground. Yellowish
Light drains from notorious eyes

Of the males, stealing their first
& last sex. The pact's outcast,
The albino we humans love,
Whimpers, wags his tail,

& crawls forward on his belly.
He never sleeps at night.
After pacing down thorny grass
Where the alpha male urinated,

A shadow limps off among the trees.
Already sentenced into wilderness,
As if born wounded, he must stand
Between man & what shines.

from *Ontario Review*

The Triumph
of Narcissus and Aphrodite

◇ ◇ ◇

Am I cool or an asshole? Check this: I'm at this artsy-fartsy faculty party wearing a mauve turtleneck, white blazer, granny glasses and a tooled-silver peace symbol on a leather thong around my neck. Perfect for this crowd, right? I figure I'll test it out. So I lay some heavy eyes on this knockout blonde, about five eight with legs up to here, and when she giggles and whispers in her girlfriend's ear, I read green and move on her, tearing a can from my six-pack. "So," I begin, popping the top, "What do you think of the new Pei student center?" The beer foams up over the edge of the can; I suck it swiftly, but not before some dribbles onto my jacket. She titters, brushing a Veronica Lake curl from her face. "O I thought it was totally awesome"—a bimbo for sure, I think, with pretensions—"Form following function but with a dramatic sweep one ordinarily finds in the work of architects intending merely to outrage the sensibilities. And," she adds, "without the stark serenity of Aalto's last works, y'know? Like the Nordic Ski Center he did for the Sibelius house." She tugs at her mini, I pull a lapel aside to show her my gut, flat and rock-hard from five workouts a week. She's got a foot-wide smile, best caps I've ever seen, skin flawless even in the glare of the floodlights. It's clear she's a cute little smartass who loves repartee, so I give her some: "Bet you don't remember Ted Williams' last game!" I go to straighten up gain an inch look even more imposing, but my back has gotten stiff. It's these new shoes, I think. And the hostess must've dimmed the lights. That's cool: more romantic. Still, she doesn't look as clear-skinned now and her smile's lost maybe a little luster. "O I don't?" she comes back, a slight tremor and something savage in her voice.

"He went four-for-four with a three-hundred-and-fifty-foot homer his last at-bat ever!" She wipes a fleck of spit from her mouth. "And I saw every Ginger Rogers–Fred Astaire movie ever made. Stood in line the night they opened. Got the ticket stubs from each one." Her neck's thrust out at me and I could swear she's got a wattle. She's trembling with rage, but you know how cool I am? Even with the sudden ache in my hands and the stiffness in my neck I manage to taunt her with something I think will stop her cold: "I useta party with Dante!" Is it getting darker? And somebody turned off the heat. Her girlfriend's gone and all the other guests, too. There's just a guy sweeping up who stops and leers at us. It pisses me off some, but I lean forward to hear her cause there's this buzz in my ears like a hive of bees, and I realize she's been yapping at me all the while. "Phaeton!" she screams, "When he drove Apollo's chariot across the sky and fell to earth in flames. I was THERE!" Her teeth are yellow and crooked, she's leaning on a stick, her clothes are rags. Now she's just an ectoplasmic outline, a gray halo in the cold dark. (Do I need a new prescription?) The walls are covered with moss. Water drips down onto the rock floor. I'm bent almost double, I can't see her at all, and all I hear is someone laughing. I stare at my shivering hand. There's my pinky ring. I'm still cool.

from *Black Warrior Review*

Nunc Dimittis

◇　◇　◇

Little time now
and so much hasn't
been put down as I
should have done it.
But does it matter?
It's all been written
so well by my betters,
and what they wrote
has been my joy.

from *DoubleTake*

The Shipfitter's Wife

◇ ◇ ◇

I loved him most
when he came home from work,
his fingers still curled from fitting pipe,
his denim shirt ringed with sweat
and smelling of salt, the drying weeds
of the ocean. I'd go to where he sat
on the edge of the bed, his forehead
anointed with grease, his cracked hands
jammed between his thighs, and unlace
the steel-toed boots, stroke his ankles
and calves, the pads and bones of his feet.
Then I'd open his clothes and take
the whole day inside me—the ship's
gray sides, the miles of copper pipe,
the voice of the foreman clanging
off the hull's silver ribs. Spark of lead
kissing metal. The clamp, the winch,
the white fire of the torch, the whistle,
and the long drive home.

from *DoubleTake*

The Sleepless Grape

◇   ◇   ◇

Like any ready fruit, I woke
falling toward beginning and
welcome, all of night
the only safe place.
Spoken for, I knew
a near hand would meet me
everywhere I heard my name
and the stillness ripening
around it. I found my inborn minutes
decreed, my death appointed
and appointing. And singing
gathers the earth
about my rest,
making of my heart a way home
the stars hold open.

from *Water Stone*

First Love

◇   ◇   ◇

It was a flower.

There had been,
before I could even speak,
another infant, girl or boy unknown,
who drew me—I had
an obscure desire to become
connected in some way to this other,
even to *be* what I faltered after, falling
to hands and knees, crawling
a foot or two, clambering
up to follow further until
arms swooped down to bear me away.
But that one left no face, had exchanged
no gaze with me.

This flower:
                    suddenly
there was *Before I saw it,* the vague
past, and *Now.* Forever. Nearby
was the sandy sweep of the Roman Road,
and where we sat the grass
was thin. From a bare patch
of that poor soil, solitary,
sprang the flower, face upturned,
looking completely, openly
into my eyes.
                    I was barely
old enough to ask and repeat its name.

"Convolvulus," said my mother.
Pale shell-pink, a chalice
no wider across than a silver sixpence.

It looked at me, I looked
back, delight
filled me as if
I, not the flower,
were a flower and were brimful of rain.
And there was endlessness.
Perhaps through a lifetime what I've desired
has always been to return
to that endless giving and receiving, the wholeness
of that attention,
that once-in-a-lifetime
secret communion.

from *Kalliope*

The Return

◊   ◊   ◊

All afternoon my father drove the country roads
between Detroit and Lansing. What he was looking for
I never learned, no doubt because he never knew himself,
though he would grab any unfamiliar side road
and follow where it led past fields of tall sweet corn
in August or in winter those of frozen sheaves.
Often he'd leave the Terraplane beside the highway
to enter the stunned silence of mid-September,
his eyes cast down for a sign, the only music
his own breath or the wind tracking slowly through
the stalks or riding above the barren ground. Later
he'd come home, his dress shoes coated with dust or mud,
his long black overcoat stained or tattered
at the hem, sit wordless in his favorite chair,
his necktie loosened, and stare at nothing. At first
my brothers and I tried conversation, questions
only he could answer: Why had he gone to war?
Where did he learn Arabic? Where was his father?
I remember none of this. I read it all later,
years later as an old man, a grandfather myself,
in a journal he left my mother with little drawings
of ruined barns and telephone poles, receding
toward a future he never lived, aphorisms
from Montaigne, Juvenal, Voltaire, and perhaps a few
of his own: "He who looks for answers finds questions."
Three times he wrote, "I was meant to be someone else,"
and went on to describe the perfumes of the damp fields.
"It all starts with seeds," and a pencil drawing
of young apple trees he saw somewhere or else dreamed.

I inherited the book when I was almost seventy,
and with it the need to return to who we were.
In the Detroit airport I rented a Taurus;
the woman at the counter was bored or crazy:
Did I want company? she asked; she knew every road
from here to Chicago. She had a slight accent,
Dutch or German, long black hair, and one frozen eye.
I considered but decided to go alone,
determined to find what he had never found.
Slowly the autumn morning warmed; flocks of starlings
rose above the vacant fields and blotted out the sun.
I drove on until I found the grove of apple trees
heavy with fruit, and left the car, the motor running,
beside a sagging fence, and entered his life
on my own for maybe the first time. A crow welcomed
me home, the sun rode above, austere and silent,
the early afternoon was cloudless, perfect.
When the crow dragged itself off to another world,
the shade deepened slowly in pools that darkened around
the trees; for a moment everything in sight stopped.
The wind hummed in my good ear, not words exactly,
not nonsense either, nor what I spoke to myself,
just the language creation once wakened to.
I took off my hat, a mistake in the presence
of my father's God, wiped my brow with what I had,
the back of my hand, and marveled at what was here:
nothing at all except the stubbornness of things.

from *The Atlantic Monthly*

DAVID MAMET

A Charade

◊   ◊   ◊

A piece of paper
Which appeared to be blank
But on which we see
Writing had faded.
"My first is of the
Possessive of those
Given to possession.
And my last, the finality
Of that proposition.
In entirety I give
That which in three worlds doth live.
Ungainly in the two;
In all, long-legged beauty,
Much as you."
Upon the paper which had come to fade
We strain to see
An ancient charade.
Can you decipher me?

from *Ploughshares*

The Swim

◇　◇　◇

The lake, wide but longer
than the imagination (it makes its own
horizon north and south), comes prettily
to our feet, a giant animal grown
gentle. Is it like anything else
we know? I remember being thirteen and
briefly in love with a boy already
as large as a large man, and him offering
his tender lips to mine—the rest of his
body there, but not touching, not yet.
Have we forgotten everything else?
If I want I can remember everything—
the not tender, the not gentle—
but look at what we're being offered,
the chance to strip down, accept grace
with our own grace, dive in and forget.

from *Poetry*

Misgivings

◇   ◇   ◇

"Perhaps you'll tire of me," muses
my love, although she's like a great city
to me, or a park that finds new
ways to wear each flounce of light
and investiture of weather.
Soil doesn't tire of rain, I think,

but I know what she fears: plans warp,
planes explode, topsoil gets peeled away
by floods. And worse than what we can't
control is what we could; those drab,
scuttled marriages we shed so
gratefully may augur we're on our owns

for good reasons. "Hi, honey," chirps Dread
when I come through the door; "you're home."
Experience is a great teacher
of the value of experience,
its claustrophobic prudence,
its gloomy name-the-disasters-

in-advance charisma. Listen,
my wary one, it's far too late
to unlove each other. Instead let's cook
something elaborate and not
invite anyone to share it but eat it
all up very very slowly.

from *Poetry* and *Poetry Daily*

The Characters
of Dirty Jokes

◇ ◇ ◇

Two weeks after the saleswoman told the farm brothers
to wear condoms so she wouldn't get pregnant,
they sit on the porch wondering if it's all right
to take them off. They are about as bewildered
as the man at the bar whose head is tiny
because he asked the fairy godmother, granter of all
wishes, for a little head. Except for a moment,
you get the feeling, none of them have been that happy
about being attached to the preposterous requirements
of the things between their legs, which, in their resting
state, even the elephant thinks are a scream.
"How do you breathe through that thing?" he asks
the naked man. What the naked man replies, looking down
with this new view of himself, the joke doesn't say,
though he's probably not about to laugh. On the other
hand, what was so funny about our own stories
as boys and girls when we heard our first ones,
suddenly wearing patches of hair that had nothing
to do with Sunday school or math class? How lovely
that just as we were discovering the new distance
between ourselves and polite society, the secret
lives of farm girls and priests were pressed
into our ears. Later, when we found ourselves
underneath house mortgages and kids' dental bills,
having taken up the cause of ideal love, they got funny
because they'd never heard of it, still worried,

say, about penis size, like the guy who had his
lengthened by the addition of a baby elephant's
trunk and was doing fine until the cocktail party
where the hostess passed out peanuts.
Their obsessions revealed at the end of their jokes,
they have always been losers, going back to Richard Nixon,
who tried oral sex but never could get it
down Pat, going all the way back to Eve,
thrown out of the Garden for making the first candy,
Adam's peanut brittle. Yet let us celebrate the characters
of dirty jokes, so like us who have made them
in the pure persistence of their desire,
the innocent wish to find a way out of their bodies.

from *Mid-American Review*

A Ball

◇ ◇ ◇

Translated from the Polish by Czeslaw Milosz and Robert Hass

He gives to the chief the head of an enemy
Whom he pounced on in the bushes by a stream
And hefted with his spear.——A scout
From the enemy village. It's a pity
It wasn't possible to capture him alive.
Then he would have been put on the sacrificial altar
And the whole village would have had a feast:
The spectacle of his being killed slowly.
They were rather tiny brown people
Presumably no more than a meter-fifty tall.
What remains of them are some ceramics,
Though they did not know the potter's wheel.
Something else, too: found in the tropical jungle
A granite ball, immense, incomprehensible.
How, without knowing iron, could they dress the granite,
Give it a perfectly spheric shape?
They worked it for how many generations?
What did it mean to them? The opposite
Of everything that passes and perishes? Of muscles, skin?
Of leaves crackling in a fire? A lofty abstraction
Stronger than anything because it is not alive?

from *Partisan Review*

FROM *Sonny's Hands*

◇   ◇   ◇

Sonny says the earth speaks to him—
a call and response—
as he tamps it with the back hoe
that they got here last summer.
Sometimes it tells him to go slowly—
and then discloses what it's hidden:
a pipe or cistern, a trove of old bottles
—or some other treasure he'll uncover
when he shuts off the machine
and gets the short-handled shovel.
"I could write your name
in the earth with that back hoe,"
he once told me—
"but I still like the feel of a tool."

It was a short-handled shovel he used
that spring, "when the ground finally thawed,"
and his "stillborn"
(as he called his child,
who'd been kept all winter in their barn)
"could finally be laid where it belonged."
He told me how he felt—
digging the earth, "so full of life—
even in that tiny hole."
And how, when he struck the rock,
he realized "that no one—
and especially not a child—
should lie forever
with such a huge, hard, lifeless thing."

He described then how he got his truck,
backed it up to the rim,
set the chains to the axle
—and gunned it till he had it out.
But turning back to the neatly tapered mound,
he could see "a hundred smaller stones"
—poking out their fists among the grains.
And though his family was already on their way,
he knelt and raked his bare hands
through that mound—
till he'd sifted out each stone, each pebble,
and scooped them all onto his plaid jacket,
and dumped them with their awful clattering
into the empty, metal bed of his truck.

But Sonny's hands didn't rest—
not even as the mourners came toward him,
bringing that thing so delicate.
He could see what would happen
—with the cardboard wrapping,
damp from the winter in the barn.
And not thinking at all—
about what *anyone* would say—
his hands
scooped up his child from the grass—
and shielding it from all their eyes
against his soiled chest,
he brought it to the earth
—and wrapped it in the blanket he had made.

from *The Southern Review*

What It Meant

◇   ◇   ◇

I didn't know what it meant that he was born
in the beauty of the lilies, maybe bulbs that had been
planted around the timbers of the stable,
or the myrrh king had brought them, or the frankincense
king. But the kings came after the birth, and he was
born in the beauty. Maybe on the longest
night of the winter he was somehow born
on Easter—born risen. I loved that he was
born across the sea, as if born into the whole
width of the air, between here
and that holy place, the barn under
the meteor. They didn't talk about the hay,
or the water-trough, or the blood, or the milk,
or the manure, with its straw-seeds inside it, but sometimes
they showed him in her arms, almost nursing,
the light around his head like a third
breast in the scene, and they said he was born
with a glory in his bosom—he had his own
bosom, as if he was his own mother
as well as his own father. And she wore
blue, always unmarked, she never wore
fleurs-de-lys, and yet he was born
in the beauty of the lilies. This morning, when I looked
at a lily, just beginning to open,
its long, slender pouch tipped
with soft, curling-back lips, and I could peek just
slightly in, and see the clasping
interior, the cache of pollen,
and smell the extreme sweetness, I thought they were

shyly saying Mary's body,
he came from the blossom of a woman, he was born
in the beauty of her lily.

from *The Southern Review*

Flare

◇　◇　◇

1.

Welcome to the silly, comforting poem.

It is not the sunrise,
which is a red rinse,
which is flaring all over the eastern sky;

it is not the rain falling out of the purse of God;

it is not the blue helmet of the sky afterward,

or the trees, or the beetle burrowing into the earth;

it is not the mockingbird who, in his own cadence,
will go on sizzling and clapping
from the branches of the catalpa that are thick with blossoms,
    that are billowing and shining,
        that are shaking in the wind.

2.

    You still recall, sometimes, the old barn on your
great-grandfather's farm, a place you visited once, and
went into, all alone, while the grownups sat and talked
in the house.

It was empty, or almost. Wisps of hay covered the
floor, and some wasps sang at the windows, and maybe there
was a strange fluttering bird high above, disturbed, hoo-ing
a little and staring down from a messy ledge with wild,
binocular eyes.

Mostly, though, it smelled of milk, and the patience
of animals; the give-offs of the body were still in the
air, a vague ammonia, not unpleasant.

Mostly, though, it was restful and secret, the roof
high up and arched, the boards unpainted and plain.

You could have stayed there forever, a small child in
a corner, on the last raft of hay, dazzled by so much
space that seemed empty, but wasn't.

Then—you still remember—you felt the rap of hunger—
it was noon—and you turned from that twilight dream and
hurried back to the house, where the table was set, where
an uncle patted you on the shoulder for welcome, and there
was your place at the table.

3.

Nothing lasts.
There is a graveyard where everything I am talking about is, now.

I stood there once, on the green grass, scattering flowers.

4.

Nothing is so delicate or so finely hinged as the wings
of the green moth
against the lantern
against its heat
against the beak of the crow
in the early morning.

Yet the moth has trim, and feistiness, and not a drop
   of self-pity.

Not in this world.

5.

My mother
was the pale blue wisteria,
my mother
was the mossy stream out behind the house,
my mother, *alas, alas,*
did not always love her life,
heavier than iron it was
as she carried it in her arms, from room to room,
oh, unforgettable!

I bury her
in a box
in the earth
and turn away.
My father
was a demon of frustrated dreams,
was a breaker of trust,
was a poor thin boy with bad luck.
He followed God, there being no one else
he could talk to;
he swaggered before God, there being no one else
who would listen.
Listen,
this was his life.
I bury it in the earth.
I sweep the closets.
I leave the house.

6.

I mention them now,
I will not mention them again.

It is not lack of love
nor lack of sorrow.
But the iron thing they carried, I will not carry.

I give them—one, two, three, four—the kiss of courtesy,
    of sweet thanks,
of anger, of good luck in the deep earth.
May they sleep well. May they soften.

But I will not give them the kiss of complicity.
I will not give them the responsibility for my life.

7.

Did you know that the ant has a tongue
with which to gather in all that it can
of sweetness?

Did you know that?

8.

The poem is not the world.
It isn't even the first page of the world.

But the poem wants to flower, like a flower.
It knows that much.

It wants to open itself,
like the door of a little temple,
so that you might step inside and be cooled and refreshed,
and less yourself than part of everything.

9.

The voice of the child crying out of the mouth of the
   grown woman
is a misery and a disappointment.
The voice of the child howling out of the tall, bearded,
   muscular man
is a misery, and a terror.

10.

Therefore, tell me:
what will engage you?
What will open the dark fields of your mind,
   like a lover,
      at first touching?

11.

Anyway,
there was no barn.
No child in the barn.

No uncle no table no kitchen.

Only a long lovely field full of bobolinks.

12.

When loneliness comes stalking, go onto the fields, consider
the orderliness of the world. Notice
something you have never noticed before,

like the tambourine sound of the snow-cricket
whose pale green body is no longer than your thumb.

Stare hard at the hummingbird, in the summer rain,
shaking the water-sparks from its wings.

Let grief be your sister, she will whether or no.
Rise up from the stump of sorrow, and be green also,
   like the diligent leaves.

A lifetime isn't long enough for the beauty of this world
and the responsibilities of your life.

Scatter your flowers over the graves, and walk away.
Be good-natured and untidy in your exuberance.

In the glare of your mind, be modest.
And beholden to what is tactile, and thrilling.

Live with the beetle, and the wind.

This is the dark bread of the poem.
This is the dark and nourishing bread of the poem.

from *Shenandoah*

And Now

◊   ◊   ◊

Yesterday toads
no bigger than houseflies
took small hops
across our path.

It would have been easy
to miss them—
under the tall trees and the charm
of the wind in their tops—
those perfectly shaped
little black toads
along the black path.

from *Acorn*

Say You Love Me

◇   ◇   ◇

What happened earlier I'm not sure of.
Of course he was drunk, but often he was.
His face looked like a ham on a hook above

me—I was pinned to the chair because
he'd hunkered over me with arms like jaws
pried open by the chair arms. "Do you love

me?" he began to sob. "Say you love me!"
I held out. I was probably fifteen.
What had happened? Had my mother—had she

said or done something? Or had he just been
drinking too long after work? "He'll get *mean*,"
my sister hissed, "just *tell* him." I brought my knee

up to kick him, but was too scared. Nothing
could have got the words out of me then. Rage
shut me up, yet "DO YOU?" was beginning

to peel, as of live layers of skin, age
from age from age from him until he gazed
through hysteria as a wet baby thing

repeating, "Do you love me? Say you do,"
in baby chokes, only loud, for they came
from a man. There wouldn't be a rescue

from my mother, still at work. The same
choking sobs said, "Love me, love me," and my game
was breaking down because I couldn't do

anything, not escape into my own
refusal, *I won't, I won't,* not fantasize
a kind, rich father, not fill the narrowed zone,

empty except for confusion until the size
of my fear ballooned as I saw his eyes,
blurred, taurean—my sister screamed—unknown,

unknown to me, a voice rose and leveled
off, "I love you," I said. *"Say 'I love you,
Dad!' "* "I love you, Dad," I whispered, leveled

by defeat into a cardboard image, untrue,
unbending. I was surprised I could move
as I did to get up, but he stayed, burled

onto the chair—my monstrous fear—she screamed,
my sister, "Dad, the phone! Go answer it!"
The phone wasn't ringing, yet he seemed

to move toward it, and I ran. He had a fit—
"It's not ringing!"—but I was at the edge of it
as he collapsed into the chair and blamed

both of us at a distance. No, the phone
was not ringing. There was no world out there,
so there we remained, completely alone.

from *Fence*

Hemingway's Garden

◇   ◇   ◇

I. DEAD MAN'S WATER

Ernest had strong convictions about trees,
and therefore when he saw his gardener
about to prune a few branches,
he stepped forward and restrained him.
Soon they got into an argument,
the gardener defending his right to prune,
saying pruning was his art, going back
thousands of years. Ernest stood firm,

saying he didn't give a damn, his trees
were not to be pruned. The Cuban
also stood firm. "A gardener," he said,
"that is what he does—he prunes!"
"Not my trees," Ernest insisted,
"I'm the boss here and you are my gardener
and my orders are that you are not to prune."
The proud gardener threw down his shears,

walked away in a huff, was soon out the gate.
When he could not find another job,
he returned, begged Ernest to take him back.
He promised not to prune a single branch,
not even a twig. Ernest just said too bad
but he had already hired another gardener,
one who does not prune. Two weeks later
buzzards circling a deep well called attention

to the unemployed gardener who had gone
straight there and leapt in, as soon
as he had left Ernest and his new gardener
who did not prune. "Why," Ernest asked
Pichilo, the new gardener, "did this man come
to kill himself at my farm, in my well?"
Pichilo assured his employer that it was not
his fault that Pedro had owned no farm
of his own, with no well for the jumping.
(These conversations come out better
in Spanish.) "I still think trees
should always be allowed to grow
without restraint, do you not agree?"

Ernest asked, and Pichilo strongly agreed.

II. The Interim Gardener

The newly-hired gardener meant no offense,
he said, but he desired to ask Ernest
just one question. Did the no-pruning rule
apply even to roots like that big one
of the ceiba tree—the root that had grown
under the house and was raising the tiles
of the floor? It was about to ruin the house.
If Señor Jeminguey did not object, he said,
he would just clip that one big root
so the tiles could fall back into place.
He was sure the tree would not mind.
Ernest replied that he thought he had made
himself quite clear, and he hoped
there was no need to lose another gardener
in one of his wells. Was that quite clear?
But one day when Ernest was in Havana,
Mary called Pichilo in, explained
that despite her "spoiled and bad-tempered
husband," the bothersome root had to be cut.
She would deal with his temper, not to worry.
The gardener did as she asked, with two

quick blows of his axe. Just then Ernest
returned. Without a word, he rushed
to his twelve gauge doublebarrelled shotgun.
The gardener jumped out the window,
ran for his life, the root still in his hand.
Ernest was right behind him, firing.
As the gardener told it years later,
Mrs. Hemingway had to perform penance
each day by kneeling before the ceiba
and asking forgiveness, saying the prayer
that her husband prescribed. Ernest watched
to make sure she did it. The famous root,
dropped by the gardener as he fled,
still hangs as a trophy over the door
of the *finca,* which is now a museum.

III. AN ABRAZO

Before he left Cuba for the last time
Ernest took a walk with Pichilo,
his gardener. "He who says goodbye
often," he quoted, "never leaves—
It's a good saying, and yet
I do not think it is true. I do not
think, my friend, that I have time—
not enough to come back again.
I feel very sick, and your Cuban
doctors can't seem to find out
what's wrong with me." Ernest
found it easy to speak bluntly
of such matters in Spanish,
to those like Pichilo who could
be trusted to say nothing for years.

With even more candor he added
a description of how his father,
the surgeon, had shot himself
with a pistol—a Smith & Wesson
.38. "I always thought my old man

was a coward," Ernest said,
"but now I know better." Pichilo
seemed to know just what
his boss meant. Then Ernest added
that neither animals nor humans
should die in bed or be allowed
to suffer or make others suffer.
"They seem to understand that
with horses well enough, but not
with the rest of us." Pichilo's
face said it all—understanding
and agreement without
and beyond words. With a last
and strong *abrazo,* hugging him
close, Ernest bid his gardener,
his friend Pichilo, *Adios,*
then shoved into his hand a wad
of Cuban money, saying
he no longer had any use for it.

from *New Millennium Writings*

Seven Skins

◇   ◇   ◇

1

Walk along back of the library
in 1952
someone's there to catch your eye
Vic Greenberg in his wheelchair
paraplegic GI—
Bill of Rights Jew
graduate student going in
by the only elevator route
up into the great stacks where
all knowledge should and is
and shall be stored like sacred grain
while the loneliest of lonely
American decades goes aground
on the postwar rock
and some unlikely
shipmates found ourselves
stuck amid so many smiles

Dating Vic Greenberg you date
crutches and a chair
a cool wit an outrageous form:
"—just back from a paraplegics' conference,
guess what the biggest meeting was about—
Sex with a Paraplegic!—for the wives—"
In and out of cabs his chair
opening and closing round his
electrical monologue the air

furiously calm around him
as he transfers to the crutches

But first you go for cocktails
in his room at Harvard
he mixes the usual martinis, plays Billie Holiday
talks about Melville's vision of evil
and the question of the postwar moment:
Is there an American civilization?
In the bathroom huge
grips and suction-cupped
rubber mats long-handled sponges
the reaching tools a veteran's benefits
in plainest sight

And this is only memory, no more
so this is how you remember

Vic Greenberg takes you to the best restaurant
which happens to have no stairs
for talk about movies, professors, food
Vic orders wine and tastes it
you have lobster, he Beef Wellington
the famous dessert is baked alaska
ice cream singed in a flowerpot
from the oven, a live tulip inserted there

Chair to crutches, crutches to cab
chair in the cab and back to Cambridge
memory shooting its handheld frames
Shall I drop you, he says, or shall
we go back to the room for a drink?
It's the usual question
a man has to ask it
a woman has to answer
you don't even think

2

What a girl I was then what a body
ready for breaking open like a lobster
what a little provincial village
what a hermit crab seeking nobler shells
what a beach of rattling stones what an offshore raincloud
what a gone-and-come tidepool

what a look into eternity I took and did not return it
what a book I made myself
what a quicksilver study
bright little bloodstain
liquid pouches escaping

What a girl pelican-skimming over fear what a mica lump splitting
into tiny sharp-edged mirrors through which
the sun's eclipse could seem normal
what a sac of eggs what a drifting flask
eager to sink   to be found
to disembody   what a mass of swimmy legs

3

Vic into what shoulder could I have pushed your face
laying hands first on your head
onto whose thighs pulled down your head
which fear of mine would have wound itself
around which of yours   could we have taken it   nakedness
without sperm   in what insurrectionary
convulsion would we have done it   mouth to mouth
mouth-tongue to vulva-tongue to anus   earlobe to nipple
what seven skins each have to molt what seven shifts
what tears boil up through sweat to bathe
what humiliatoriums   what layers of imposture

What heroic tremor
released into pure moisture

might have soaked our shape   two-headed   avid
into your heretic
linen-service
sheets?

from *The Progressive*

Writing from Memory

◇   ◇   ◇

My father got up and put on his dress.
It's the Fifties and there are stockings,

The kind with lines that go up like a part
In the thick hair of his calf.

He adjusts his bra like anyone
And we don't think much of it this morning

When he misses the catch and asks for help.
He bends over and looks through the closet

Picking out a right-colored pair of shoes,
Something he knows from memory in that dimness

Pale enough to match his purse.

My mother doesn't get up, not right away, not easy
Making some noise as she lies there

Rubbing her hand across the thick stubble of her face.
She asks if her brown trousers are clean,

But nobody answers, and she shakes her head.
As she gets up she puts a hand inside her underwear

Rubbing a buttock hard.
She puts on a sleeveless tee-shirt

Then a shoulder holster, but no gun,
Not before breakfast. We've all agreed on that one.

And for God's sake, we say, brush your teeth.

My sister puts on her jeans and after zipping up
She moves her thing around as if anyone cares

Until she gets it just right, to the side of the seam.
She keeps leaving the toilet seat up

And walking around the house without a shirt on
To show her pecs off. She flexes one for me

That little bounce looking like a wink.

Then there's me. The golden boy, the good
Reader. Oh yeah, I was perfect

Is what I remember.
I would pull on a cotton blouse

Blue, with a neat, pleated skirt,
Then a sweater. I held my books up to my chest.

It made my parents feel better.
The day started. We were off, to our jobs,

To Coronado Elementary School, to whatever was next.
Finally, we just got in the family car

And drove it straight out of the Fifties.
By the end of the century we'd be different people.

We'd be fond of saying Those days don't seem real anymore.
And it's true.

We've forgotten all of this about each other.
Now when we talk about who we were

We tell some other family's story.

from *Meridian*

That Will to Divest

◇ ◇ ◇

Action creates
a taste
for itself.
Meaning: once
you've swept
the shelves
of spoons
and plates
you kept
for guests,
it gets harder
not to also
simplify the larder,
not to dismiss
rooms, not to
divest yourself
of all the chairs
but one, not
to test what
singleness can bear,
once you've begun.

from *The Yale Review*

Last recording session/for papa joe

◇   ◇   ◇

don't be so mean papa
cuz the music don't come easily now
don't stomp the young dude
straining over his birthright.
he don't know what he doing yet
his mornings are still comin
one at a time
don't curse the night papa joe
cuz yo beat done run down
we still hear yo fierce tides
yo midnight caravans singing tongues into morning.
don't be so mean man
one day he'll feel the thunder in yo/hands
yo/arms wide as the sea
outrunning the air defiantly.
you been ahead so long
can't many of us even now
follow the scent you done left behind.
don't be so mean man un less
you mean
   to be mean
     to be
       me
   when you mean
     to be
       mean.

from *Painted Bride Quarterly*

REVAN SCHENDLER

The Public
and the Private Spheres

◇ ◇ ◇

—Prague, 1992–94

How much of you
must I withhold,
forget, that you
have sung to me
as to a child,
that I have watched
you grating onions,
shared your tears?
Have I seen you,
lying near, limbs
twitching in release,
was I dreaming
of a conversation
about the pacts we make
with foreign forces,
how we are ready to subvert
our talent or our outrage
for a measure of certainty,
and what recompense
there is, if any,
for time we've spent
detained, repeating
what so many have done

before us? What of those
disfigured hours waiting
to reveal the details
of unremarkable days:
must we count them as lost?
Could you?
It would seem
we both can, and do,
with diplomatic ease,
just as we turn our ears
and eyes from those
calling out so clearly to us
from the next room.
Then let's forget together,
dear, there's nothing
we can really do.

from *Salmagundi*

Longing and Wonder

◇   ◇   ◇

"Talk to Myra you talk to the wall,"
Mama announced when I lived

so long in my head. Behind
my lids was where I fit.

O world, be small enough to hold me,
slow enough to let me swallow.

Maybe I belonged back inside her. Or
beneath the spine of a book. Maybe

among tall buildings to incubate
between their legs. The warm kitchen

was never for me though I wanted
to shine. *Passion* I called

the pressure wrestling underneath.
Yesterday, in an audience listening to

my first book of poems,
a full professor asked me: "Longing,

how is it different from wonder?"
Astonished, jack-lit as a robber

caught with the goods, I felt my eyes
struggle to withdraw—and then

in longing you close your eyes,
but in wonder you open them.

When those words went
ZINGing through the lovely room,
you bet your sweet ass they opened.

from *Common Sense*

CHARLES SIMIC

Barber College Haircut

◊   ◊   ◊

In my head thrown back as in a nose bleed,
There are, of course,
A dozen or so replicas of myself,
Much reduced, wearing hoods perhaps.

They sit at the same table
With a conspiratorial air debating
The baffling question of my identity,
The unresolved pros and cons

Shuffled back and forth like a deck
Of smutty postcards. Embracing couples
In haystacks, on hotel beds,
Moonlit beaches at night, saloons—

The grim reaper buying me a drink—
What the hell is going on here, I said?
At which the barber rushed over
And threw a hot towel over my eyes.

From *AGNI*

A Shearling Coat

◇   ◇   ◇

Alexander Ortiz and Arlyne Gonzales
were walking home from a movie.

A car drew up, and two men
got out. One had a gun, the other

tugged at her shearling coat.
"Don't hurt her," Ortiz said, "she's pregnant."

The gunman shot him twice,
in the chest and throat.

"What you do that for?" said the other.
"C'mon, c'mon, get the jacket,"

the gunman said, and they left,
with a shot at Gonzales.

She had thrown herself down
on top of the dying man.

And I shall be wanting to be rid
of this thing till the end of my days.

from *The Hudson Review*

THOMAS R. SMITH

Housewarming

◇   ◇   ◇

In my dream I was the first to arrive
at the old home from church. Wind
and night had forced through the cracks.
I pushed inside, turned on lamps,
lit a fire in the stove. Frozen oak
logs stung my fingers; it was good
pain, my hands reddening on the icy
broom-handle as I swept away snow.
On Christmas Eve, I prepared a warm
place for my mother and father, sister
and brothers, grandparents, all my relatives,
none dead, none missing, none angry
with another, all coming through the woods.

from *AGNI*

A Star Is Born
in the Eagle Nebula

◇　◇　◇

to Larry Levis, 1946–1996

They've finally admitted that trying to save oil-soaked
seabirds doesn't work. You can wash them, rinse them
with a high-pressure nozzle, feed them activated charcoal
to absorb toxic chemicals, & test them for anemia, but the oil
still disrupts the microscopic alignment of feathers that creates
a kind of wet suit around the body. (Besides, it costs $600 to wash
the oil slick off a penguin & $32,000 to clean an Alaskan seabird.)
We now know that the caramel coloring in whiskey causes nightmares,
& an ingredient in beer produces hemorrhoids. Glycerol
in vodka causes anal seepage, & when girls enter puberty,
the growth of their left ventricles slows down for about a year.
Box-office receipts plummeted this week. Retail sales are sluggish.
The price of wheat rose. Soybeans sank. The Dow is up thirty points.
A man named Alan Gerry has bought Woodstock & plans
to build a theme park, a sort of combo Williamsburg-Disneyland
for graying hippies. The weather report predicts a batch of showers
preceding a cold front down on the Middle Atlantic Coast—
you aren't missing much. Day after day at the Ford research labs
in Dearborn, Michigan, an engineer in charge of hood latches
labors, measuring the weight of a hood, calculating the resistance
of the latch, coming up with the perfect closure, the perfect snapping
sound, while the shadow of Jupiter's moon, Io, races across cloud tops
at 10.5 miles a second, and a star is born in the Eagle Nebula.

Molecular hydrogen and dust condenses into lumps that contract
and ignite under their own gravity. In today's paper four girls
in a photo appear to be tied, as if by invisible threads, to five
soap bubbles floating along the street against the black wall
of the Park Avenue underpass. Nothing earthshattering. The girls
are simply *there*. They've blown the bubbles & are following them
up the street. That's the plot. *A life. Any life.* I turn the page
and there's Charlie Brown. He's saying, "Sometimes I lie awake
at night & ask, Does anyone remember me? Then a voice
comes to me out of the dark—'Sure, Frank, we remember you.' "

from *The Gettysburg Review* and *Poetry Daily*

Ways to Live

◇   ◇   ◇

19–21 July

1 INDIA

In India in their lives they happen
again and again, being people or
animals. And if you live well
your next time could be even better.

That's why they often look into your eyes
and you know some far-off story
with them and you in it, and some
animal waiting over at the side.

Who would want to happen just once?
It's too abrupt that way, and
when you're wrong, it's too late
to go back—you've done it forever.

And you can't have that soft look when you
pass, the way they do it in India.

2 HAVING IT BE TOMORROW

Day, holding its lantern before it,
moves over the whole earth slowly
to brighten that edge and push it westward.
Shepherds on upland pastures begin fires
for breakfast, beads of light that extend
miles of horizon. Then it's noon and
coasting toward a new tomorrow.

If you're in on that secret, a new land
will come every time the sun goes
climbing over it, and the welcome of children
will remain every day new in your heart.
Those around you don't have it new,
and they shake their heads turning gray every
morning when the sun comes up. And you laugh.

3 BEING NICE AND OLD

After their jobs are done old people
cackle together. They look back and shiver,
all of that was so dizzying when it happened;
and now if there is any light at all it
knows how to rest on the faces of friends.
And any people you don't like, you just turn
the page a little more and wait while they
find out what time is and begin to bend
lower; or you can turn away
and let them drop off the edge of the world.

4 GOOD WAYS TO LIVE

At night outside it all moves or
almost moves—trees, grass,
touches of wind. The room you have
in the world is ready to change.

Clouds parade by, and stars in their
configurations. Birds from far
touch the fabric around them—you can
feel their wings move. Somewhere under
the earth it waits, that emanation
of all things. It breathes. It pulls you
slowly out through doors or windows
and you spread in the thin halo of night mist.

from *Cream City Review*

PEGGY STEELE

The Drunkard's Daughter

◊   ◊   ◊

I got drunk in college once
and crazy. Turned over to a friend
I could trust, I found a line
that held great meaning.
My father walked the town.
My father walked the town.
It seemed deeper than all Shakespeare.

from *Blue Sofa*

RUTH STONE

A Moment

◇　◇　◇

Across the highway a heron stands
in the flooded field. It stands
as if lost in thought, on one leg, careless,
as if the field belongs to herons.
The air is clear and quiet.
Snow melts on this second fair day.
Mother and daughter,
we sit in the parking lot
with doughnuts and coffee.
We are silent.
For a moment the wall between us
opens to the universe;
then closes.
And you go on saying
you do not want to repeat my life.

from *Paterson Literary Review*

Deer Crossing the Sea

◇　◇　◇

Many things were like sleep,
wholly in the power of the forest,
the deep middle, deep shiver, deep shade,
from which many things ran, unawake,
in search of new mountains to graze,
covered in flowers, *my love, I am sick,*
or covered in snow, pink with algae,
in search of impossible light
made of water, whose sapphire waves
swathed their heads, *you were only a dream,*
as they swam out to meet it, kicking their hooves,
no longer breathing, because no one
or nothing can quit once the body gets wind
of an eden—the promise of nectar
haunts them forever, the shore pecked out
of their eyes, and there, in its stead,
something greater to catch,
a scent that would paralyze God.

from *Green Mountains Review*

The Minefield

◇　◇　◇

He was running with his friend from town to town.
They were somewhere between Prague and Dresden.
He was fourteen. His friend was faster
and knew a shortcut through the fields they could take.
He said there was lettuce growing in one of them,
and they hadn't eaten all day. His friend ran a few lengths ahead,
like a wild rabbit across the grass,
turned his head, looked back once,
and his body was scattered across the field.

My father told us this, one night,
and then continued eating dinner.

He brought them with him—the minefields.
He carried them underneath his good intentions.
He gave them to us—in the volume of his anger,
in the form of a stick, a belt,
in the bruises we covered up with sleeves,
In the way he threw anything against the wall,
a radio, that wasn't even ours,
a melon, once, opened like a head.
In the way we still expect, years later and continents away,
that anything might explode at any time,
and we would have to run on alone
with a vision like that
only seconds behind.

from *Tor House Newsletter*

Thoreau and the Crickets

He found them bedded in ice, in the frozen puddles
    Among reeds and clumps of sedges in the marsh:
        House and field crickets lying near the surface
On their sides or upside down, their brittle hind legs
    Cocked as if to jump as free as fiddlers
        In the final rain before winter. The ice
Had clarified the brown and green shades
    Of their chitin and magnified
        The thickened radiant veins of the forewings
On which they'd made their music
    Those nights when he'd listened, half-asleep,
        To their creaking, their wise old saws
That told him over and over they were with him
    And of him down to the vibrant depths
        Of his eardrums and canals and the foundation
Of his house on earth. With his heels and hands
    He broke the puddles around them carefully,
        Cracking them loose and filling his coat pockets
With fragments like clear glass, holding them hard
    As fossils in shale. He would take them home
        And learn from them, examine their lost lives
With scales and ruler, tweezers and microscope.
    He would bring them back to order and pay homage
        To all they'd been and left undone. He strode
Briskly and happily through the crusted lanes
    And slipped through the paths of town, delighted
        To be alive all winter, to be ready
And able to warm their spirits with his own,
    But on his doorstep, reaching into his coat,

He lifted out, dripping with snow-melt,
Two hands full of wriggling, resurrected crickets
    Crawling over each other, waving and flexing
        Antennae and stiff legs to search his palms
For another springtime. For a while, he held them
    And watched them wriggle drunkenly
        And scrabble in half-death for what they imagined
He had to give, then put them gently
    Again into his pockets and carried them
        Back through the snow and ice to their cold beds.

from *Ploughshares*

This Pleasing Anxious Being

◇   ◇   ◇

I

In no time you are back where safety was,
Spying upon the lambent table where
Good family faces drink the candlelight
As in a manger scene by de La Tour.
Father has finished carving at the sideboard
And Mother's hand has touched a little bell,
So that, beside her chair, Roberta looms
With serving bowls of yams and succotash.
When will they speak, or stir? They wait for you
To recollect that, while it lived, the past
Was a rushed present, fretful and unsure.
The muffled clash of silverware begins,
With ghosts of gesture, with a laugh retrieved,
And the warm, edgy voices you would hear:
Rest for a moment in that resonance.
But see your small feet kicking under the table,
Fiercely impatient to be off and play.

II

The shadow of whoever took the picture
Reaches like Azrael's across the sand
Toward grownups blithe in black-and-white, encamped
Where surf behind them floods a rocky cove.
They turn with wincing smiles, shielding their eyes
Against the sunlight and the future's glare,

Which notes their bathing caps, their quaint maillots,
The wicker picnic hamper then in style,
And will convict them of mortality.
Two boys, however, do not plead with time,
Distracted as they are by what?—perhaps
A whacking flash of gull wings overhead—
While off to one side, with his back to us,
A painter, perched before his easel, seeing
The marbled surges come to various ruin,
Seeks out of all those waves to build a wave
That shall in blue summation break forever.

III

Wild, lashing snow, which thumps against the
    windshield
Like earth tossed down upon a coffin lid,
Half clogs the wipers, and our Buick yaws
On the black roads of 1928.
Father is driving; Mother, leaning out,
Tracks with her flashlight beam the pavement's edge,
And we must weather hours more of storm
To be in Baltimore for Christmastime.
Of the two children in the back seat, safe
Beneath a lap robe, soothed by jingling chains
And by their parents' pluck and gaiety,
One is asleep. The other's half-closed eyes
Make out at times the dark hood of the car
Plowing the eddied flakes, and might foresee
The steady chugging of a landing craft
Through morning mist to the bombarded shore,
Or a deft prow that dances through the rocks
In the white water of the Allagash,
Or, in good time, the bedstead at whose foot
The world will swim and flicker and be gone.

from *The New Yorker*

Archetypes

◇ ◇ ◇

Often before have our fingers touched in sleep or half-sleep and
    enlaced,
often I've been comforted through a dream by that gently sensitive
    pressure,
but this morning, when I woke your hand lay across mine in an
    awkward,
unfamiliar position so that it seemed strangely external to me,
    removed,
an object whose precise weight, volume and form I'd never
    remarked:
its taut, resistant skin, dense muscle-pads, the subtle, complex
    structure,
with delicately elegant chords of bone aligned like columns in a
    temple.

Your fingers began to move then, in brief, irregular tensions and
    releasings;
it felt like your hand was trying to hold some feathery, fleeting
    creature,
then you suddenly, fiercely, jerked it away, rose to your hands and
    knees,
and stayed there, palms flat on the bed, hair tangled down over your
    face,
until with a coarse sigh almost like a snarl you abruptly let yourself
    fall
and lay still, your hands drawn tightly to your chest, your head
    turned away,
forbidden to me, I thought, by whatever had raised you to that
    defiant crouch.

I waited, hoping you'd wake, turn, embrace me, but you stayed in
    yourself,
and I felt again how separate we all are from one another, how even
    our passions,
which seem to embody unities outside of time, heal only the most
    benign divisions,
that for our more abiding, ancient terrors we each have to find our
    own valor.
You breathed more softly now, though; I took heart, touched
    against you,
and, as though nothing had happened, you opened your eyes,
    smiled at me,
and murmured—how almost startling to hear you in your real
    voice—"Sleep, love."

from *Ontario Review*

CHARLES WRIGHT

American Twilight

◊   ◊   ◊

Why do I love the sound of children's voices in unknown games
So much on a summer's night,
Lightning bugs lifting heavily out of the dry grass
Like alien spacecraft looking for higher ground,
Darkness beginning to sift like coffee grains
                                        over the neighborhood?

Whunk of a ball being kicked,
Surf-suck and surf-spill from traffic along the by-pass,
American twilight,
                    Venus just lit in the third heaven,
Time-tick between "Okay, let's go," and "This earth is not my home."

Why do I care about this? Whatever happens will happen
With or without us,
                    with or without these verbal amulets.
In the first ply, in the heaven of the moon, a little light,
Half-light, over Charlottesville.
Trees reshape themselves, the swallows disappear, lawn sprinklers do the wave.

Nevertheless, it's still summer: cicadas pump their boxes,
Jack Russell terriers, as they say, start barking their heads off,
And someone, somewhere, is putting his first foot, then the second,
Down on the other side,
                    no hand to help him, no tongue to wedge its weal.

from *Partisan Review*

TIMOTHY YOUNG

The Thread of Sunlight

◇ ◇ ◇

Where the thread of sunlight crossed the top bunk,
I touched the rough-cut rafter,
and watched two spiders approach
on the lumber's vertical plane.

Just when my heart condensed to arachnid size
the great wounds of war opened before me.
One spider limped on,
with the other's head in its mouth.

When I asked my mother about war,
she told me, "You're thinking too much and . . ."
Before her sentence ended my father rushed in,
chattering about the chores we'd accomplish.
The magneto for the mill saw needed repair,
the window trim should be painted,
the outboard motors could be tuned,
and if the work gets done,
we might go fishing in the evening.

The sunlight reflected off the flat lake
and I stood, between my mother
and father, thinking.

from *The Journal of Family Life*

CONTRIBUTORS' NOTES AND COMMENTS

DICK ALLEN was born in Troy, New York, in 1939 and grew up in the tiny village of nearby Round Lake, where his father was postmaster, a gas station attendant, and writer on early American technology and transportation. After graduation from Syracuse and Brown universities, Allen edited *The Mad River Review* at Wright State University and then moved to the University of Bridgeport, where he has taught senior seminars, international literature, and creative writing since 1968. He is director of creative writing and Charles A. Dana Endowed Chair Professor of English at the university. The most recent of his nine books is *Ode to the Cold War: Poems New and Selected* (Sarabande Books, 1997). He has received fellowships from the National Endowment for the Arts and the Ingram Merrill Foundations, and poetry awards from the Poetry Society of America and *Poetry*.

Allen writes that "the special issue of *The Café Review* in which 'The Selfishness of the Poetry Reader' appeared was devoted to Donald Hall, one of our century's chief poetry readers and lovers.

"I was trying to capture the apartness that men, especially, may feel when they love poetry in a non-poetry-loving age. As the poetry reader speaks, this love turns into pride, defiance, hyperbole, exaggeration. Yet I hope the poem's speaker evokes how poetry is pervasive throughout the lives of its readers. I wanted those who don't regularly abandon themselves to reading poetry to know something of what they're missing.

"The poem, additionally, is a way of paying tribute to some of the modern poets and poems I love, including two poetry collections key to my own work. Aside from poets actually named, there are references or allusions to works by Andre Vosnesensky, Sylvia Plath, Wallace Stevens, W. D. Snodgrass, Elizabeth Bishop, Robert Bly, Karl Shapiro, Richard Wilbur, William Carlos Williams, Randall Jarrell, W. H. Auden.

"The poem ends in a Donald Hall dark house, emphasizing secrecy and seriousness. I also had in mind the famous Randall Jarrell appreciation of Robert Frost, 'To the Laodiceans,' where Jarrell writes of Frost's poetry, 'The grimness and awfulness and untouchable sadness of things, both in the world and in the self, have justice done to them in the poems, but no more justice than is done to the tenderness and love and delight; and everything in between is represented somewhere too. . . .'

"In effect, the selfish poetry reader speaking this poem says that poetry is much more dangerous than politics and that you can't be a real Marlboro man unless you read poetry. I love that. Take *that,* my small-town boy companions! Take that, my father, who—until he reached his eighties—thought poetry was only for girls!

"My wife and I felt a great sense of relief when, in their adulthood, both our daughter and our son became regular poetry readers."

JOHN BALABAN was born in Philadelphia in 1943. A volume of new and selected poems, *Locusts at the Edge of Summer* (Copper Canyon, 1997), was a finalist for the National Book Award and won the William Carlos Williams Prize from the Poetry Society of America. Next year, Copper Canyon will publish his *Spring Essence: The Poetry of Ho Xuan Huong,* a Vietnamese woman who lived around 1800. He teaches at the University of Miami.

Of "Story," Balaban writes: "A true story. Almost a found poem. The quotes are direct quotes. For years I kept the man's business card, thinking I ought to send him the poem, although I never did. He lived on a planet where people always paid if they took something from you and I think I feared he might ask money for using his story. Anyway, I was touched by his love for his dead son. This was many years ago. Maybe he picked me up because of his son."

COLEMAN BARKS was born in Chattanooga, Tennessee, in 1937. He is best known for his translations of Rumi as published in *The Essential Rumi* (Harper, 1995) and *The Glance* (Viking, 1999). Four volumes of his own poetry have appeared. He is emeritus professor of poetry at the University of Georgia.

Barks writes: "Bill Matthews died suddenly in November 1997. I have heard that he was getting ready to go out to the opera. If you don't know his poetry, don't feel ashamed for long. Go and buy the *Selected Poems and Translations, 1969–1991* (Houghton Mifflin). His great, generous, elegant, raffish, and tender laugh is there in the poems and will help keep us sane."

GEORGE BILGERE was born in St. Louis, Missouri, on July 4, 1951. He teaches English at John Carroll University in Cleveland. He has taught English as a Second Language in Tokyo and was a 1991 Fulbright Scholar in Bilbao, Spain. From 1989 to 1991 he taught at the University of Oklahoma. He has received grants in poetry from the National Endowment for the Arts and the Ohio Arts Council. In 1994 his first book of poetry, *The Going,* was published by the University of Missouri Press and received the Devins Award. His second book, *Big Bang,* was published by Copper Beech Press in 1999. Charles Simic selected a poem of his for *The Best American Poetry 1992.*

Of "Catch," Bilgere writes: "My father was a gifted baritone but his career ended when he lost a lung to tuberculosis when he was thirty. Eventually he became the president of a large automobile dealership in St. Louis but that was plainly not a world he loved or was well suited to; he moved through the realms of business deals and negotiations at a certain distance. I remember him sitting in his office, looking up from the contracts piled on his magnificent mahogany desk to listen to the voice of Jussi Björling pouring from the radio. He was equally distracted as a father; I never quite had his attention, but on rare occasions he would attempt some traditional demonstration of fatherly love. 'Catch' describes such a moment."

ELIZABETH BISHOP (1911–1979) was born in Worcester, Massachusetts, grew up in New England and Nova Scotia, and was educated at Vassar College. She lived in New York, Paris, Key West, Mexico, Washington, D.C. (as Consultant in Poetry at the Library of Congress from 1949 until 1951) and, for nearly twenty years, in Rio de Janeiro, Petropolis, and Ouro Preto, Brazil. Her books include *North & South* (1946); *Poems: North & South—A Cold Spring* (1955, Pulitzer Prize); *Questions of Travel* (1965); *The Complete Poems* (1969, National Book Award), and *Geography III* (1976). She also translated *The Diary of "Helena Morley"* (1957), wrote, "with the editors of *Life,*" the *Life* World Library *Brazil* (1962), and was co-editor of *An Anthology of Twentieth-Century Brazilian Poetry* (1972). Her posthumous volumes include *The Complete Poems 1927–1979* (1983) and *The Collected Prose* (1984), both edited by Robert Giroux and published by Farrar, Straus, and Giroux. *One Art,* a volume of her selected letters, appeared in 1994.

Alice Quinn notes that "Foreign-Domestic" is among the many previously unpublished poems to be found in the author's notebooks and papers bequeathed to the Vassar College Library. The poem is undated, "but Bishop's longtime editor, Robert Giroux, says that 'eye-fee' would be the local pronunciation of 'hi-fi' in Brazil, where Bishop lived with her companion, Lota de Macedo Soares."

CHANA BLOCH was born in New York City and educated at Cornell, Brandeis, and the University of California at Berkeley. She has published three books of poems: *The Secrets of the Tribe* (Sheep Meadow Press, 1981), *The Past Keeps Changing* (Sheep Meadow Press, 1992), and *Mrs. Dumpty* (University of Wisconsin Press, 1998), which was selected by Donald Hall for the 1998 Felix Pollak Prize in Poetry. Her translations from Hebrew include the biblical Song of Songs and books by the Israeli poets Yehuda Amichai and Dahlia Ravikovitch. She has also written a study of the seventeenth-century English poet George Herbert, *Spelling the Word* (University of California Press, 1985). She has received two fellowships from the National Endowment for the Arts and one from the National Endowment for the Humanities. She lives in Berkeley and is currently W. M. Keck Professor of English Literature and Director of the Creative Writing Program at Mills College in Oakland, California.

Of "Tired Sex," Bloch writes: "How does one articulate in poetry the truth about a failed relationship—the real truth, as we say, to distinguish it from the other one? In this poem the twin tongs of wit and metaphor enable me to handle what would otherwise be too hot to touch.

" 'Tired Sex' comes from my new book, *Mrs. Dumpty*, which tells the story of the life and death of a long marriage. The speaker is sober, middle-aged, and stripped of her illusions, though she has held on to her sense of humor. I think of this poem as salty and funny at the same time—a mixture I value in many of the writers I like best.

"Metaphor is the great enabler, the agent of transformation. In the process of spinning misery into poetry, the poet finds herself transformed. What happened in bed is better forgotten; when the poem remembers, what happens on the page may become a source of pleasure."

PHILIP BOOTH was born in Hanover, New Hampshire, in 1925 and attended Dartmouth College and Columbia University. Viking Penguin has published all ten of his books of poems, including, most recently, *Selves* (1990) and *Pairs* (1994). "Narrow Road, Presidents' Day" appears in *Lifelines: Selected Poems, 1950–1999*. In 1996 *Trying to Say It* was published in the University of Michigan Press's Poets on Poetry series. He has received many honors for his work, including fellowships from the Guggenheim Foundation and the National Endowment for the Arts. For twenty-five years, ending in 1986, he taught at Syracuse University. He now lives in Maine.

Of "Narrow Road, Presidents' Day," Booth writes: "The poem was catalyzed by the woman leaning out her back window, watching two horses; it was in fact Presidents' Day, and so there was a sniff of spring. Two miles *beyond* the woman I saw three heavy sheep in a sheep pen. As I kept driving, I saw the remains of the same road-kill porcupine I'd seen smushed the past Sunday.

"Returning home, I saw the dead skunk, and began to know I had to start writing. Upstairs, I leaned on my desk to make notes, and drafted some lines that seemed right for what the poem was beginning to want. My notebook now tells me that the poem went through twenty-three draft sheets in February, and ten more in early March. All told, I got hearing what the poem gave me."

JOHN BREHM was born in Lincoln, Nebraska, in 1955. A graduate of the University of Nebraska and Cornell University, he has taught at Emerson College, Portland State University, Marylhurst College for Lifelong Learning, and most recently as a visiting writer at Cornell. His poems have appeared in *Poetry, The Southern Review, The Gettysburg Review, New England Review, Poetry Northwest,* and *Epoch.* Currently, he lives in New York City and works for Oxford University Press.

Brehm writes: "Since its originating circumstances are related in the poem itself I'll just say here that during the period when I wrote 'Sea of Faith' I was trying to use dialogue as a way to get other voices, other people, into my poems. Formally, I wanted to see if elements of the sonnet structure could be transferred to longer, free verse poems—in this case the buildup of tension and the 'turn' toward its release one finds in traditional sonnets. I recall also that I was reading Frank O'Hara at the time and keeping an eye out for comic possibilities in my own work. But mostly I was having fun at someone else's expense and then realizing that, of the two of us, she was in the far more enviable, though irretrievable, position."

HAYDEN CARRUTH was born in Waterbury, Connecticut, in 1921. He is currently living in retirement in upstate New York. He has published forty books of poetry, essays, and fiction, the most recent being *Beside the Shadblow Tree* (Copper Canyon Press, 1999).

Carruth writes: "The poem 'Because I Am' was commissioned by an organization of scholars and enthusiasts for the centennial celebration of Sidney Bechet's birthday in New Orleans in 1997. Although I had been deeply moved by music almost from infancy, Bechet was the first musician to whom I paid close attention, beginning in the early 1930s. On his best records he remains the consummate jazzman. I never tire of listening to him."

LUCILLE CLIFTON was born in Depew, New York, in 1936. She is the mother of six grown children and the author of poetry, prose, and assorted books for children. Her first book of verse, *Good Times,* appeared in 1969. She went on to publish such collections as *An Ordinary Woman* (1974), *Two-Headed Woman* (1980), *Next* (1987), *The Book of Light* (Copper Canyon Press, 1993), and *The Terrible Stories,* which reflects on her survival of breast cancer. In 1999 she received a writer's award from the Lila Wallace–Reader's Digest Fund. She was also elected to the Board of Chancellors of the Academy of American Poets. She is Distinguished Professor of Humanities at St. Mary's College of Maryland.

Of "the mississippi river empties into the gulf," Clifton writes: "This is a poem about connections and so is about everything."

BILLY COLLINS was born in New York City in 1941. His recent books include *Picnic, Lightning* (University of Pittsburgh Press, 1998), *The Art of Drowning* (University of Pittsburgh Press, 1995)—a finalist for the Lenore Marshall Prize—and *Questions About Angels* (William Morrow, 1991), which was selected by Edward Hirsch for the National Poetry Series and reprinted by the University of Pittsburgh Press in 1999. He has won the Bess Hokin Prize, the Frederick Bock Prize, the Oscar Blumenthal Prize, and the Levinson Prize awarded by *Poetry* magazine. A recipient of a Guggenheim fellowship and a grant from the National Endowment for the Arts, he is a professor of English at Lehman College (City University of New York) and a visiting writer at Sarah Lawrence College. He lives in northern Westchester County.

Of "Dharma," Collins writes: "For years I had no dog. Or, as I liked to think of it, I was 'between dogs.' Nonetheless, every so often a dog would appear in one of my poems. I might be writing about taking a walk or spending the day at home, and a dog would unexpectedly lope onto the scene. If anyone would ask me about the dog, I would always admit that it was just a 'poetry dog.' But now I have the real thing, a little collie mix, who was the inspiration for the poem and whose name, by the way, is not Dharma, but Jeannine after the title of a very upbeat tune by Cannonball Adderly. The poem itself, I think, is about as self-explanatory as they come—almost as self-explanatory as the dog herself."

ROBERT CREELEY was born in Arlington, Massachusetts, in 1926. He is a New Englander by birth and disposition, although he has spent most of his life in other parts of the world, including Guatemala, British Columbia, France, and Spain. In the 1950s he taught at Black Mountain College and also edited *The Black Mountain Review*, a crucial gathering place for alternative senses of writing at that time. Charles Olson, then rector of the college, Robert Duncan, and Edward Dorn are among the company he met there. Subsequently he taught at the University of New Mexico and in 1966 went to the State University of New York at Buffalo, where he still teaches as the Samuel Capen Professor of Poetry and the Humanities. Although usually identified as a poet (*For Love, Pieces, Windows,* and *Selected Poems* are examples of his many collections), he has written a significant body of prose, including a novel, *The Island,* and a collection of stories, *The Gold Diggers,* all of which is to be found in *The Collected Prose of Robert Creeley.* His critical writings are published in *The Collected Essays of Robert Creeley,* and his correspondence with Charles Olson is now in ten volumes and continuing (*The Complete Correspondence*). His most recent poetry collections are *Life & Death* and *So There.* He was awarded the Bollingen Prize in poetry in 1999; the judges were Carolyn Kizer and Gary Snyder. He was New York State Poet from 1989 to 1991.

Of "Mitch," Creeley writes: "After seventy, the prospect of death is real indeed—but it is still a shock when a friend dies. It is as if a neighborhood were inexplicably emptying, lights going out in all the windows. I had known Mitchell Goodman since our time at Harvard in the early forties. My meeting Denise Levertov was a consequence of their marriage in the late forties. The friend who told me of Mitch's illness was the poet Hilda Morley, from Black Mountain days, who had had the bleak information from Denise. It is Hilda's 'whispered information.' Now all three are dead."

LYDIA DAVIS was born in Northampton, Massachusetts, in 1947 and lives in upstate New York with her husband and son. She is the author of *Break It Down* (1986), *The End of the Story* (1995), and *Almost No Memory* (1997), all published by Farrar, Straus & Giroux. She has been the recipient of several awards, including, most recently, a Lannan Literary Award. She has translated numerous books from the French and is currently working on a new translation of Proust's *Swann's Way (Du côté de chez Swann)* for Penguin Classics.

Davis writes: "Another 'betrayal': I think that my mother is flirting with a man from her past who is not my father. I say to myself: Mother ought not to have improper contacts with this man 'Franz'! She met 'Franz' some decades ago. He is a European. But this is an example of the 'old reality' coexisting in my brain alongside the 'new reality.' My reaction came bobbing up to the surface immediately: She ought not to see this man in an improper way while Father is 'away'! But my father will not be returning home; he now resides at Vernon Hall. My mother herself is ninety-four years old. There can be no improper relations with a woman of ninety-four, surely. Yet there is still some confusion: her capacity for subversion and betrayal is quite young and fresh, if her body is not."

DEBRA KANG DEAN was born in Honolulu, Hawai'i, in 1955 and received an MFA from the University of Montana in 1989. A contributing editor for *Tar River Poetry* and a student of the Magic Tortoise Taijiquan School in Chapel Hill, North Carolina, she lives in Lincoln, Massachusetts, with her husband, Bradley P. Dean, and their two cats. Her essay, "Telling Differences," is included in *Under Western Eyes: Personal Essays from Asian America* (Anchor Books, 1995), and her chapbook, *Back to Back* (NCWN, 1997), won the Harperprints chapbook poetry competition. "Taproot" is included in her first full-length collection of poems, *News of Home* (BOA Editions Limited, 1998).

Of "Taproot," Dean writes: "In early 1998, I had the opportunity to work for a week with elementary school children in Bertie County, North Carolina. On the second day, I took in a wonderful book called *Play with Your Food*. 'What is it?' I asked, not quite sure what their response would be to the first picture I showed them. A few children raised their hands; I called on one. 'Uh, squash?' she answered tentatively. I nodded. 'What is it?' I asked again. A brief pause and then, 'Geese, geese!' several children shouted, waving their hands and, to my delight, breaking the raise-your-hand-and-wait-to-be-called-on rule of the classroom. 'Yes, both!' I said. So it is with metaphor. Sometimes one is not quite sure the made thing will settle in the groove between squash and geese, vehicle and tenor, and be both things at once. It was the bias of my mentor and friend Peter Makuck against poems about poetry that challenged me to explore more fully the possibility of extended metaphor, to try to have it both ways.

"What 'Taproot' is about and the way it discovers its ending in relation to its apparent subject is, I hope, clear enough that it needs no comment from me. And yet, knowing myself to be my father's daughter, I will acknowledge that early on in the writing of it, I was being implicated in—and maybe redeemed by—this ars poetica poem. As someone who writes poetry, I'm finding that what matters increasingly to me is the ongoing process of creating out of the materials at hand, however homely they are, 'palpable designs' not on the reader, but on the poem itself. The body that, in stooping, remembered more than I knew is proving a good teacher."

CHARD DENIORD was born in New Haven, Connecticut, in 1952. He is the author of *Asleep in the Fire* (University of Alabama Press, 1990). For the past nine years he has taught comparative religions, philosophy, and English at the Putney School in Vermont. He currently teaches English and creative writing at Providence College. He lives in Westminster West, Vermont, with his wife, Liz, and her deaf springer spaniel, Zola.

Of "Pasternak," deNiord writes, "I have been thinking about Pasternak ever since seeing David Lean's *Dr. Zhivago* in New York around Christmastime when I was twelve in 1965. This experience became a Proustian memory for me. Julie Christie as Lara became my 'magic lantern.' As a country boy from Bedford County, Virginia, I was beguiled by both the grandeur of the New York theater and the exotic romance of the movie. But it was Dr. Zhivago's avocation as a poet that I was drawn to most powerfully. I blurred the line between Zhivago and Pasternak, learning later when I began to read Pasternak's poetry in college that his heartbreak had been close enough to his heroic doctor's. As I began to contemplate the direction of my adult life, I developed an increasing interest in Pasternak the man vis-à-vis Zhivago. His example as an exiled writer in his own country, a Russian genius under Soviet rule, loomed larger and larger. I was particularly in awe of what Emily Dickinson would have called his "adequate" gift for two genres: he was able to complement his poetry with an epic novel, for which he won the Nobel Prize. Akhmatova in her elegy for him wrote that he had 'been rewarded by a kind of eternal childhood, / with the generosity and brilliance of the stars; / the whole of the earth was his to inherit, / and his to share with every human spirit' (Stanley Kunitz's translation). It wasn't until I reached my mid-forties that I felt inclined to write something about him myself.

There were difficulties that Pasternak himself had anticipated. In an interview with Olga Carlisle in 1960, he commented, 'My generation found itself naturally the focal point of history. Our works were dictated by the times. They lack universality now that they have aged. I believe that it is no longer possible for lyrical poetry to express the immensity of our experience. Life has grown too cumbersome, too complicated.' "

RUSSELL EDSON lives in Connecticut with his wife, Frances. His books of poetry include *The Very Thing that Happens* (New Directions, 1964), *What a Man Can See* (The Jargon Society, 1969), *The Childhood of an Equestrian* (Harper & Row, 1973), *The Reason Why the Closet-Man Is Never Sad* (Wesleyan, 1977), *With Sincerest Regrets* (Burning Deck, 1980), *The Wounded Breakfast* (Wesleyan, 1985), *Tick Tock* (Coffee House Press, 1992), and *The Tunnel: Selected Poems* (Oberlin College Press, 1994). He is also the author of *The Falling Sickness,* a collection of plays (New Directions, 1975), and two novels: *Gulping's Recital* (Guignol Books, 1984) and *The Song of Percival Peacock* (Coffee House Press, 1992).

Edson writes: " 'Pure' poetry is silence."

LAWRENCE FERLINGHETTI was born in Yonkers, New York, in 1919. Following his undergraduate years at the University of North Carolina in Chapel Hill, he saw service in the U.S. Navy as a ship's commander in World War II. After working briefly for *Time* magazine, he received a master's degree from Columbia in 1947 and a doctorate from the Sorbonne in 1950. In 1953 he founded, with Peter D. Martin, City Lights, the first all-paperbound bookstore in the country, and by 1955 had launched City Lights Books. His publication of Allen Ginsberg's *Howl* in 1956 led to his arrest on obscenity charges, and the trial that followed (he was acquitted) brought national attention to San Francisco Renaissance and Beat movement writers. *A Coney Island of the Mind* (1958) has had an enduring popularity and has been translated into nine languages. In August 1998 he was named San Francisco's poet laureate. His latest book is *A Far Rockaway of the Heart* (New Directions, 1998).

Of "A Buddha in the Woodpile," Ferlinghetti writes: "The poem has to stand (or fall) by itself. If it has to be explained, explicated, or footnoted, it is a failure as a communication. The Buddha in any woodpile cannot be explained."

DAN GERBER was born near Fremont, Michigan, in 1940. He taught high school English and later taught at Michigan State and at Grand

Valley State universities. In the late sixties and early seventies, with Jim Harrison, he edited a literary magazine called *Sumac.* He worked in business and, for five years, in his early twenties, was a professional racing driver. His first novel began as what he believed to be a poem and went long. His third novel, *A Voice from the River,* a collection of short stories called *Grass Fires,* and *A Last Bridge Home: New & Selected Poems* were all published by Clark City Press. His poems have appeared in *The Nation, The New Yorker, The Georgia Review,* and *Exquisite Corpse,* and he has written for *Sports Illustrated, Outside, New York, Men's Journal,* and other magazines. Michigan State University Press will publish his sixth collection of poems, *Trying to Catch the Horses,* in the fall of 1999. He divides his time between Key West, Florida, and the Idaho/Wyoming border.

Of "My Father's Fields," Gerber writes: "My father, Daniel F. Gerber, a sergeant in the 126th Infantry, returned from World War I a highly decorated soldier before celebrating his twentieth birthday. He never talked much about his war experiences and neglected even to tell his parents he had received the Croix de Guerre. Occasionally I could pry a story out of him. He told me no one could appreciate what a war is like if they didn't know the smell of it. He told me the most vivid image he carried away from his experience was that of fields covered with dead horses. He told me with some bitterness that if the combatants had been allowed to make the settlement after the war, they would have been a great deal more humane than the politicians. 'We didn't hate the Germans,' he said. 'We knew what they'd been through.'

"A decade after my father's death, I took his journal from 1918 on a pilgrimage of sorts and followed his movements around France. From his description, I found the grave of his friend, Carl Johnson, on a hill between the graves of two aviators, one French and one German, though an old man in the village told me the bodies had been moved after the war. Then, several years ago, I read *The Last Days of Innocence: America in 1918* by Marion and Susie Harries, and a story about a heroic act by eight volunteers from the Michigan National Guard, one of whom, it turned out, was my father, made the hair on the back of my neck stand up. The next day I wrote the first draft of 'My Father's Fields.' "

LOUISE GLÜCK was born in New York City in 1943. She is the author of nine books of poetry, including *Vita Nova* (Ecco, 1999), her latest. *Proofs and Theories,* a collection of her essays, appeared in 1994. She has received the National Book Critics Circle Award (for *The Triumph of*

Achilles), a William Carlos Williams Award, a PEN/Martha Albrand Award for nonfiction, and the Pulitzer Prize for *The Wild Iris* (Ecco, 1992). She was the guest editor of *The Best American Poetry 1993*. The poem anthologized in this year's *Best American Poetry* is the opening poem in her new volume. In 1999 she was elected to The Board of Chancellors of the Academy of American Poets.

Of "Vita Nova," Glück writes: "The truth is, I can't remember anything about how this poem was written. I know that the last lines had been with me for a very long time with no setting. The same is true of the first line."

RAY GONZALEZ was born in El Paso, Texas, in 1952. He has an endowed chair, the McKnight Land Grant Professorship, at the University of Minnesota, where he teaches creative writing and literature. He received an MFA in creative writing from Southwest Texas State University. He is the author of five books of poetry, including *The Heat of Arrivals* (BOA Editions, 1996), winner of a PEN/Oakland Josephine Miles Book Award, and *Cabato Sentora* (BOA Editions, 1999). In 2000, the University of Arizona Press will publish his cultural memoir, *Turtle Pictures*. He is also the editor of twelve anthologies, most recently *Touching the Fire: Fifteen Poets of the Latino Renaissance* (Anchor/Doubleday Books, 1998). He has served as poetry editor of *The Bloomsbury Review* for eighteen years and recently founded a new poetry journal, *LUNA.*

. Gonzalez writes, "As I discovered the secret history of my mother's side of the family, strange things happened in my poetry. As my grandmother slowly revealed her Yaqui background, 'Breastbone' began to take shape as one of the first clues to where this side of my family came from. While working on a number of poems about northern Mexico and hidden origins, I read a newspaper article about Yaqui shamans who still roamed the mountains of San Luis Potosi, Mexico. One account told of a shaman who, years ago, healed a boy bitten by a rattlesnake. Years later, this boy had become the village shaman and was now recounting many tales that had been locked in the canyons and arroyos of his native land. 'Breastbone' is an attempt to bring these secrets across international borders, admitting that my Chicano/U.S. upbringing had a great deal to do with the distance between family history and my life as an American poet. The goal with 'Breastbone' and its companion poems in my recent book, *Cabato Sentora,* has been to bridge the gap through language and understanding. The poem also answered several mysteries about a long sequence of rattlesnake poems

I completed several years ago. Those poems, based on recurring dreams about rattlers I had for years, led to 'Breastbone' and encountering Llaga."

JOHN HAINES was born in Norfolk, Virginia, in 1924. From 1954 to 1969 he homesteaded in Alaska, at Mile 68, Richardson Highway, southeast of Fairbanks. His books include *Fables and Distances: New and Selected Essays* (1996), *A Guide to the Four-Chambered Heart* (1996), *Collected Poems* (expanded edition, 1996), and a memoir, *The Stars, the Snow, the Fire* (1989). Twice named a Guggenheim Fellow, he has also received awards from the American Academy of Arts and Letters (1995) and the Academy of American Poets (1997). He lives in Helena, Montana, with his wife, Joy.

Haines writes: " 'The Last Election' was originally conceived in response to the 1992 presidential campaign, but was long delayed in completion. When I finished the poem I sent a copy to a fellow poet and critic, who remarked that he liked the poem very much and would like it even better if it was true! The poem happens to be one of the best I have written in the past four or five years with a political theme. It may say something about the current state of poetry in the United States that I have encountered sporadic difficulty in placing such poems. That is, political content, or comment, in poetry appears not to be welcome in most journals."

DONALD HALL was born in New Haven, Connecticut, in 1928. In 1975 with his wife, the late Jane Kenyon, he moved to a family farm in New Hampshire. He makes his living as a freelance writer, publishing children's books, magazine pieces later collected into books, short stories, and poems. His twelfth poetry collection, *Without,* appeared in 1998 from Houghton Mifflin. He was the guest editor of *The Best American Poetry 1989.*

Of "Smile," Hall writes: "When I write most of my poems of place, the land is New Hampshire's. 'Smile' is a different sort of poem of place, presenting the habits and language of a suburban culture. Working at it, I found myself concentrating on the point of view, trying to find an intimate, generalized voice, to speak the rhythms and tone of a class and a moment characterized by hypocrisy. Also, I wanted to mix the bizarre and the banal, a combination I find banal and bizarre.

" 'Smile' began as prose but kept turning into lines, into cadences and repetitions that lines can accommodate more handily than paragraphs. In a desultory fashion, with long interruptions, I worked on it for ten years. I finished it while my wife was ill but then continued to tinker with it. This version differs slightly from the one published in *The Yale Review*."

JENNIFER MICHAEL HECHT was born in New York City in 1965. She earned her Ph.D. in the history of science from Columbia University in 1995 and is a professor of history at Nassau Community College. She is a coauthor of *Western Civilization: The Continuing Experiment* (Houghton Mifflin, 1998), and has published articles on modern European philosophy and science in such journals as *French Historical Studies, The Journal of the History of the Behavioral Sciences,* and *Isis: The Journal of the History of Science Society.* She is working on a book on the history of atheism. Her poetry manuscript *The Next Ancient World* awaits a publisher. She lives among her Tonka trucks and old maps in the East Village of New York City.

Of "September," Hecht writes: "Some things are consistent to the human animal but most things are not. A historian's job really is to figure out the truth of what life was, so you have to give a lot of thought to what part of your weird human heart is determined by your cultural context and what part is basically human—so human that you could guess why Alexander ran alongside the chariots on the way to war; you know exactly that feeling, Hellenistic or otherwise: that's glory, that's knowing the perfectly shaped power of your profound talent and riding on it right into battle, certain that it will take you to each absolute decision as each decision surprises even you. But I cannot similarly guess from my universal gut what he thought about girls. That part is historically contingent.

"This poem and, actually, a lot of my poems, is about that. The way you can sit there, miserable, and every person you can think of seems miserable, A is jealous of her boyfriend, B has just been put on Depakote, and C has a cat. Which is to say that life seems gross and frustrating and you feel certain that happiness or satisfaction isn't real. At least you're not singled out for misery, at least it's endemic and egalitarian. And then you remember some night when the touch of your bodies felt like the agony of precision and your lover kept doing and saying everything you craved just at that moment. And there are moments of such joy in writing this, and sometimes in looking out my window onto First Avenue. And if all of that is true, that no one is happy and yet there is happiness, that the human heart changes more than you'd ever expect and yet it also runs alongside its chariot, blooming sweat and pounding away with the same glory that I feel right now, then it might also be true that we were once about twenty-one years old and standing outside my parents' house, and it was autumn, we were in college near my hometown and you were picking me up for a class that we were taking together and I carried my camera around a lot back then, largely because I was inspired by the photo album you and Mary had compiled back when you two were together. At that age nostalgia seemed beautiful and I wanted to create my own. (I could not have known how strange nostalgia would become.) So I have this picture of you, under the tree, leaves everywhere, drinking from one of my parents' mugs. I guess we used to bring the mugs into the car and then return them at the end of the day. I guess we were alive, and I am alive, and the person in the photograph is you."

BOB HICOK was born in Michigan in 1960. His books include *The Legend of Light* (University of Wisconsin Press, 1995), which Carolyn Kizer chose as the winner of the Felix Pollak Prize in poetry and which was an ALA Booklist Notable Book of the Year. A new volume is entitled *Plus Shipping* (BOA Editions, 1999). He received a fellowship from the National Endowment for the Arts in 1999. He owns a die design firm in Ann Arbor, Michigan.

Of "What Would Freud Say?" Hicok writes: "It's safer to be stupid in a poem with power tools and affection than in life with fire and gasoline. This would be my slogan if T-shirts were bigger. Not only did I approach the gas cap with lighter in hand, I did so proudly, convinced of the subtlety of my solution. Sanity, my sometime companion, intervened. I keep a Zippo on my desk. Because from time to time I get an idea, it remains unfilled."

JANE HIRSHFIELD was born in New York City in 1953. Her most recent books are *The Lives of the Heart,* her fourth collection of poems, and a collection of essays, *Nine Gates: Entering the Mind of Poetry,* both published by HarperCollins in 1997. She has received fellowships from the Guggenheim and Rockefeller Foundations, the Poetry Center Book Award, the Bay Area Book Reviewers Award, and other honors. She teaches in the graduate writing program at Bennington College. She lives in the San Francisco bay area.

Of "The Envoy," Hirshfield writes: "One of poetry's gifts is the way that the poetic mind can sieve the realm of outer event for images and acts that, seen deeply into, release inner life into view. The outer reaches inward, and the inner reaches back, takes hold, steps forward. Something new becomes knowable then, and both realms enlarge, increase in richness. The writer—and perhaps a reader?—is transformed. 'The Envoy,' for me, embodies this way of poem-making. The visitations of rat and then snake were quite real, as is the account of my response. But these creatures are also archetypal, and the shock of finding them inside the cabin where I was staying—and wondering, as I did, what might enter next—awakened in me a fresh sense of the utter permeability of self. We are vulnerable. Creatures, emotions, events beyond our control come and go. It is terrifying to be so defenseless, so exposed. . . . Still, that permeability to the other is the source of our happiness as well as our losses. The snake startled and frightened me, but it also thrilled. And one thing more: it gave me the poem. The mystery of what enters our lives may not be controllable or tamable, but it can be belled by our human attention. The wide leather strap of the language-herdsman can be buckled onto its neck, and in the darkness where inner and outer life commingle we can listen, in amazement, to the sounds of what we ourselves are. "

JOHN HOLLANDER was born in New York City in 1929. He has published eighteen books of poetry here and abroad, the most recent being *Figurehead and Other Poems* (Knopf, 1999), and eight critical works among which are *The Work of Poetry* (Columbia University Press, 1997) and *The Poetry of Everyday Life* (University of Michigan Press, 1998). He has been the recipient of the Bollingen Prize, the Levinson Prize, and a MacArthur Fellowship. He is Sterling Professor of English at Yale University and lives in Connecticut. He was guest editor of *The Best American Poetry 1998*.

Hollander writes: " 'Beach Whispers' is a little annotation to what seems to be an ongoing project in American poetry of trying to understand what the sounds of natural noise are saying in languages not our own. The ocean beaches of New Jersey, Long Island, and Massachusetts I have known since childhood remain significant places for me, and I think of shorelines as poetic regions where the sea of what I know but don't know that I do meets the land of what I intend and construct—where dreaming touches making. Since the sounds of nature can at best seem homonymic to words in English, it should not be embarrassing to confess that the first and second parts of this poem seem to have emerged from three punning monosyllables. In the case of whirr/*were*, serf/*surf* and sole/*Sol* the italicized homonyms are themselves only ancillary whispers, in this poem, to the primary words, but the whole matter of the poem grew from my listening to them, as if they were natural mutterings of the words—unitalicized—themselves. The first two were in my head, the way a rhythm, a form, an image can be, from the beginning. Whatever allegory this brief meditation developed emerged from trying to make sense out of them as well."

AMY HOLMAN was born at Overlook Hospital in Summit, New Jersey, in 1963 and grew up in Berkeley Heights, Summit, and down at sea level in Avalon and Stone Harbor. A graduate of the College of Wooster in Ohio, she has since lived in New York City—lately, Brooklyn—with her gregarious golden retriever. Cofounder of the Publishing Seminars at Poets & Writers, she also directs the Literary Horizons program and writes a column, "Amy Holman's Tough-Love Guide to Publishing," for *Poets & Writers* magazine. She was the associate editor for *The First Book Market* (Macmillan, 1998). She has a trio of chapbooks from Linear Arts: *Dwelling with Fire* (1997), *Tissue and Bone* (1998), and *The Cathedral of My Head* (1998).

Of "Man Script," Holman writes: " 'Our leader' was Andrei Codrescu, editor of the literary journal *Exquisite Corpse,* and there were thirty of us at the gallery five years ago. We also wrote with each other's hands on banana skins.

"It made a funny story long before I found a way to write it. It was when I was playing around with the roots of words and looking forward to an art class in manuscript illumination that it clicked. But I should've been looking for a new apartment and a friend from California had to go to a memorial service in D.C. and used my place that weekend as a hub, so I had these stolen hours to work on it when she wasn't there and I was avoiding my frustrating search. The hardest part of writing 'Man Script' was in preventing the whole, detailed experience from infringing on the poem and in keeping the balance between language and the body."

DAVID IGNATOW was born in Brooklyn, New York, in 1914 and spent most of his life in New York City. His many books include *At My Ease: Uncollected Poems of the Fifties and Sixties* (BOA Editions), *I Have a Name* (1996), *Against the Evidence: Selected Poems, 1934–1994* (1994), and *Whisper the Earth* (1981). From 1980 to 1984 he was president of the Poetry Society of America. He received the Bollingen Prize, two Guggenheim Fellowships, the Shelley Memorial Award (1996), and the Frost Medal

(1992). He died in November 1997 at his home in East Hampton, New York.

In a memorial in *American Poet,* Robert Bly writes that "David Ignatow was that strange thing—a genius disguised as a businessman. Whitman, by contrast, was a genius disguised as a genius. They were reckless father and sober stepson. David had descended deeper into the American experiment, having run a printing shop south of Houston for years, and he knew industrial labor well." Bly adds that Ignatow was a devoted father: "He always worried that his business and writing would take too much time from his children. I remember being at their apartment on upper Broadway in the early sixties. When Yaedi was young, David and Rose wanted to be with her all the time. He felt guilty to sit down at his typewriter and type poems, even late at night. All the time Yaedi was small he worried about that. Years later, Yaedi sent me her first book of poems, published perhaps when she was seventeen. In one of her poems she said something to the effect that the most important thing in her childhood was seeing her father sit down every night and write down his feelings and emotions. So we never know what will help our children. All we can do is follow depth wherever it leads. In later years Virginia Terris was there to meet him, and that was a great blessing for David."

In his poem "The Signal," Ignatow writes: "How can I regret my life / when I find the blue-green traffic light / on the corner delightful against the red brick / of my house. It is when the signal turns red / that I lose interest. At night / I am content to watch the blue-green / come on again against the dark / and I do not torture myself / with my shortcomings."

GRAY JACOBIK was born in Newport News, Virginia, in 1944. She received her undergraduate degree from Goddard College and her advanced degrees from Brandeis University. She teaches literature at Eastern Connecticut State University. Her latest books include *The Double Task,* winner of the Juniper Prize (University of Massachusetts Press, 1998), and *The Surface of Last Scattering,* winner of the X. J. Kennedy Poetry Prize (Texas Review Press, 1999).

Jacobik writes: "When I wrote 'The Circle Theatre' I was thinking about the confluence of personal and public events, and then, at times, how the spiritual and the erotic are layered into our experience as well. While all this is going on, and the human psyche integrates these various dimensions of existence into a seamless whole, the physical world is present in its everlasting cyclical way, trees and flowers in bloom, the light of the sun coming and going. This is a subject that fascinates me: how we make a whole out of the complexity and variousness, the ongoingness of experience. Of course I hoped for resonance when I mentioned De Sica's glorious film *The Garden of the Finzi-Continis*. For many years, the Circle Theatre in Washington, D.C., was the one theater in town that would show foreign and art films, and the run would last as long as people continued to come. This masterpiece, about a Jewish family living in Italy during a period of oppressive Fascist persecution, was rich in detail, filmed in that slow, sensuous, vivid, and delicious manner characteristic of some of the greatest European films of the fifties, sixties, and seventies. I wanted the erotic experience that was unfolding above the film's showing to serve as yet another layer of existence that must, somehow, be taken into account—in this case, the intersection of art and life. I could say interpenetration, for as the man is penetrating the woman, the personal, historical, natural, spiritual and artistic realms are impinging on the being of these two."

JOSEPHINE JACOBSEN was born in 1908 in Coburg, Canada, of American parents. The most recent of her ten books of poetry, *In the Crevice of Time* (Johns Hopkins University Press, 1995), received the William Carlos Williams Award and was nominated for a National Book Award. She has also received the Lenore Marshall Award, the Shelley Memorial Award, and a fellowship from the Academy of American Poets. She has published several collections of short fiction and essays, including her collected stories, *What Goes Without Saying* (Johns Hopkins University Press, 1996). She served two terms as Poetry Consultant to the Library of Congress and is currently a Literary Lion of the New York Public Library. In 1994 she was inducted into the American Academy of Arts and Letters. *The Instant of Knowing,* a volume of her lectures and criticism edited by Elizabeth Spires, was published by the University of Michigan Press in 1997. Her work appeared in the 1991 and 1993 editions of *The Best American Poetry.* She lives in Baltimore.

Of "Last Will and Testament," Jacobsen writes: "I am particularly interested in this poem, as it is one of the few poems of mine in which reality is directly transposed to paper. It is a longer poem than I usually write and has a special place in my affections."

LOUIS JENKINS was born in Oklahoma City, Oklahoma, in 1942 and grew up in Oklahoma and Kansas. He has worked as a farmhand, ranch hand, oil field worker, truck driver, librarian, commercial fisherman, and at other jobs. He is married and has one son. He has lived in Duluth, Minnesota, since 1971. His books of poetry include *Nice Fish: New and Selected Prose Poems* (1995) and *Just Above Water* (1997), both from Holy Cow! Press.

Jenkins writes: "Both 'The Fishing Lure' and 'The Life of the Poet' come from moments of 'awakening,' not in any mystical or religious sense but just from suddenly becoming aware of what I am doing (fishing, writing poetry) instead of doing things automatically, as usual, and from then asking myself 'How did I get here? Where have I been?' "

MARY KARR was born in a part of southeast Texas called the Golden Triangle in 1955. She is the author of *The Liar's Club,* a memoir (Viking, 1995), and three books of poems: *Abacus* (Wesleyan University Press, 1987), *The Devil's Tour* (New Directions, 1993), and *Viper Rum* (New Directions, 1998). She has received a Bunting Fellowship from Radcliffe College and a Whiting Writer's Award. She teaches at Syracuse University.

Of "The Patient," Karr writes: "This is probably the last elegy for my father, though he has been dead ten years and will doubtless stay dead."

X. J. KENNEDY was born in Dover, New Jersey, in 1929. He now lives in Lexington, Massachusetts, where for a living he writes children's books, some of them together with his wife, Dorothy. *Nude Descending a Staircase* (Doubleday, 1961) was his first book of verse; *Dark Horses* (Johns Hopkins University Press, 1992) his most recent. Among his textbooks is *An Introduction to Poetry, Ninth Edition* (Longman, 1998), coauthored with Dana Gioia.

Kennedy writes: " 'A Curse on a Thief' is a true story. The fisherman, my nephew Paul, had his beloved tackle box stolen from a dock in Fox Lake, Wisconsin. A very Christian gentleman, not even a beer drinker as the poem imagines him to be, Paul would never have uttered such a terrible curse in a million years, so I took the liberty of doing it for him. For inspiration, I drew on those bloodcurdling poetic damnations by medieval Welsh and Irish bards, reportedly capable of skinning the hide right off an enemy at long range."

GALWAY KINNELL was born in Providence, Rhode Island, in 1927. He received a BA at Princeton and an MA at the University of Rochester. His early books include *The Book of Nightmares* (1971) and *The Avenue*

Bearing the Initial of Christ into the New World (1974). He won the Pulitzer Prize in 1983. *Imperfect Thirst,* his latest collection of poems, was published by Houghton Mifflin in 1994. The Ecco Press will bring out *The Essential Rilke,* translated with Hannah Liebmann, in fall 1999. Kinnell lives in New York City and Vermont. He was the state poet of Vermont for a four-year term expiring in 1993 when Louise Glück succeeded him and was succeeded in turn, four years later, by Ellen Bryant Voigt. They were the first three to hold the position after Robert Frost, who remained the state poet of Vermont for several decades following his death.

CAROLYN KIZER was born in Spokane, Washington, in 1925 and was educated in Spokane public schools. Her father was a noted civil liberties lawyer and urban planner. She has three children and is married to John Woodbridge, FAIA, also a city planner. She graduated from Sarah Lawrence College in 1945, and then was a fellow of the Chinese government at Columbia University; she subsequently went to China, where her father directed Chinese relief. With Richard Hugo, she founded the poetry quarterly *Poetry Northwest* in 1959. She was the first director of literature for the National Endowment for the Arts. Her most recent collection is *Harping On: Poems 1985–1995* (Copper Canyon Press, 1996). She edited *The Essential Clare* (1992) and *100 Great Poems by Women* (1995), both published by Ecco Press. She won the Pulitzer Prize in 1985 for *Yin: New Poems* (BOA Editions, 1984).

Of "The Erotic Philosophers," Kizer writes: "I was staying with the Very Reverend James Parks Morton and his wife, Pamela, at the deanery of the Cathedral of St. John the Divine, when I picked up Peter Brown's superb biography of Augustine, which prompted my renewed interest in the saint. And one day I was in our Paris apartment when the phone rang and the caller asked if I was busy. I replied, 'I'm just sitting here drinking kir and reading Kierkegaard.' Bingo! When I find myself talking pentameter—with rhymes—I know I'm in the throes of a poem.

"St. A. and S.K. were the favorites of my teacher at Sarah Lawrence, Charles Trinkaus. In the forties I wrote a poem for him called 'I Dreamed I Was St. Augustine.' (Later I thought briefly of suing Bob Dylan for swiping it from my college literary magazine, but gave up the idea.) I also wrote a poem about Kierkegaard, an undoubted masterpiece, which I lost. To bring this deluge of memories, combined with the two great philosophers, into a poem, took me a year during which I wrote nothing else. I think of adding this work as the end piece to perhaps my best-known work, 'Pro Femina,' and finishing it once and for all. Although its ending seems a bit pallid and submissive for an old ironclad feminist like me."

RON KOERTGE was born in Lawrenceville, Illinois, in 1940. He has taught at the city college in Pasadena since 1965. Many of his early books of poems were from independent presses such as Sumac and Red Hill. In 1991 he received a National Endowment for the Arts Fellowship and a California Arts Council grant two years after that. His most recent book of poems, *Making Love to Roget's Wife*, appeared in 1997 from the University of Arkansas Press, which will publish his new book, *Geography of the Forehead*, in late 1999. He is the author of nine novels for young adults and a teacher at Vermont College in their residency MFA Writing for Children program. He adds, "By the way, my last name is pronounced as if it were Kur-chee, with the accent on the first syllable. So that mystery is solved."

Of "1989," Koertge writes: "It's been quite a few years since a pal of mine died, and although his name and memory cropped up in my work I was never quite satisfied that Jack would like the poem. That was my benchmark. Then recently a friend of mine told me how the guide dogs behaved at a funeral her daughter had attended. That was it. The minute I got home, I picked up a pen. I think Jack would like '1989.' It's a compact chronicle of the plague years, but it makes people laugh, too. I'm glad I didn't muck this poem up by trying to write it too soon or too fast. I'm not usually big on patience, but it really is a virtue, just as my mother said."

YUSEF KOMUNYAKAA was born in Bogalusa, Louisiana, in 1947. In 1969 and 1970 he served with the United States Army in Vietnam. He was a correspondent and editor of *The Southern Cross*. In 1985, he began teaching creative writing and literature at Indiana University. At present he teaches at Princeton University. He won the 1994 Pulitzer Prize and the Kingsley Tufts Award for *Neon Vernacular*. He also received the 1994 William Faulkner Prize (Université de Rennes). His other books include *Copacetic* (1984), *I Apologize for the Eyes in My Head* (1986), *Dien Cai Dau* (1988), *Magic City* (1992), and most recently *Thieves of Paradise* (Wesleyan/New England, 1998). A collection of his prose entitled *Blue Notes* is forthcoming in the University of Michigan Press's Poets on Poetry series. In 1999 he was elected to The Board of Chancellors of the Academy of American Poets.

Of "Scapegoat," Komunyakaa writes: "I feel like I've always known the scapegoat. In the amorphous human arena, that world which encompasses the sacred and profane, the surreal and pragmatic, the spectral and tangible, he personifies downfall. He is an instant Punch-n-Judy for the human ego. He's our bad guy; our dreamt up sacrifice that annuls guilt. We heap our worst thoughts on him, as he tests our conscience. He becomes our excuse to continue business as usual. When we thrash him up the hills, we are doing it for a common good: thus, the scapegoat becomes a Christ figure. He shoulders the cross, our symbolic burden, and our indebtedness (whether acknowledged or unacknowledged) becomes his reward. Such a figure undermines and/or diminishes his scapegoatness if he protests his status. He must remain the unconscious brute, a Minotaur in the labyrinth, and our duty and silent agreement is to pursue him. The scapegoat is condemned; standing 'between man & what shines,' he must guard the gems and gold, the riches and illusions, and thus dies a ritual death. In defiance of contradiction, he is a visionary who accepts the challenge to drive the money lenders and the masters of usury from the temple, the holy place. He is blessed and cursed in the same breath; the only way he is allowed to survive is to have his spirit corrupted, whereby he joins the crowd to single out another scapegoat. I believe that man's psyche embraces this target, even to the extent that we make ourselves into his image. I realize, Christian or otherwise, woman or man, a scapegoat is a scapegoat."

WILLIAM KULIK was born in Newark, New Jersey, in 1937 was raised in Philadelphia, and had his rough edges smoothed at Columbia, where his studies left him with a knowledge of language and literature a mile wide and an inch deep. In 1962, he discovered surrealism and "pataphysics," two huge abiding influences on his sense and sensibility. Among his books are *The Selected Poems of Robert Desnos* (with Carolyn Forché) (Ecco Press, 1991), *The Selected Poems of Max Jacob* (scheduled for publication by Field), and *Night and Day: Poems in Verse and Prose*.

Of "The Triumph of Narcissus and Aphrodite," Kulik writes: "The poem employs the pseudobiographical 'I' (Max Jacob's invention) in the person of a narrator whose 'cultural style'—his idiom, his allusions, the rhythms of his speech—brand him a jerk. (Just consider the way he frames his choices in the opening line.) In the lengths both the 'cat' and the 'chick' are made to go to impress each other in this take on the vanity of the pickup game, they become examples of the 'everyday surreal'—that bizarre reality that defies reason, proportion, and harmony (to mention just a few classical ideals), a reality we've not only gotten used to but in fact expect, even *demand*. Think of the immense popularity of daytime TV 'real-life' stories: Oprah, Sally Jessy, and—worst of all—Jerry Springer. Or of the millions who watched a woman so-called journalist interview another woman whose sole claim to fame was that she performed fellatio on a president. The poem tries to mirror that surreality in its mix—or clash, if you like—of allusions. Kind of like driving down a country road and seeing on one side an old stone farmhouse with a perfectly restored bank barn and on the other a strip mall. Now that's humor, late-late-twentieth-century-American style."

JAMES LAUGHLIN, the founder and longtime editor-in-chief of New Directions, was born in Pittsburgh in 1914. An heir of his family's iron and steel business, which became the Jones and Laughlin Steel Corporation, the young man attended Choate (where he studied with Dudley Fitts) and Harvard, where he majored in Latin and Italian. He met Gertrude Stein in Paris and spent six months in Rapallo, Italy, studying at Ezra Pound's "Ezuversity." In 1935 Pound persuaded the young man to give up his poetic ambitions and do "something useful," like publishing. New Directions was the direct result of Pound's advice. The small publishing house that Laughlin founded specialized in masterpieces that were unconventional, controversial, or seemingly unmarketable. *New Directions in Prose and Poetry* (1936), the first book Laughlin published, was an anthology comprising works by Pound, Elizabeth Bishop, Marianne Moore, Gertrude Stein, Wallace Stevens, and others. New Directions was Vladimir Nabokov's first U.S. publisher. Laughlin also published William Carlos Williams, Henry Miller, Dylan Thomas, Delmore Schwartz, Djuna Barnes, and many others. "It is better," Laughlin wrote, "to be read by eight hundred readers and be a good writer than be read by all the world and be Somerset Maugham." Laughlin's own *New and Selected Poems* is available from New Directions. He died at eighty-three in November 1997.

DORIANNE LAUX was born in Augusta, Maine, in 1952. She is the author of two collections of poetry from BOA Editions, *Awake* (1990) and *What We Carry* (1994), which was a finalist for the National Book Critics Circle Award. She is also coauthor, with Kim Addonizio, of *The Poet's Companion: A Guide to the Pleasures of Writing Poetry* (Norton, 1997). She has received a fellowship from the National Endowment for the Arts. She is at work on a libretto with composer Wally Brill, as well as on a new book of poems tentatively entitled *Music in the Morning.* She is the director of the University of Oregon's program in creative writing.

Of "The Shipfitter's Wife," Laux writes: "This poem about a pipefitter returning home from work, and the woman who loves him, was written by invitation for Edward Hirsch to run in the Labor Day edition of *The New York Times.* It was then rejected by the *Times'* editors as 'too racy for their readership.' Hirsch saved the poem, and later published it in an issue of *DoubleTake.* My gratitude to Robert Bly for reprinting it here."

LI-YOUNG LEE was born in Jakarta, Indonesia, in 1957 and now lives in Chicago with his wife and children. His most recent book is *The Winged Seed: A Remembrance* (Hungry Mind Press, 1999). His first book, *Rose* (1968), won the Delmore Schwartz Memorial Poetry Award, and his second, *The City in Which I Love You* (1990), was the Lamont Poetry Selection for 1990. Both books were published by BOA Editions. He has received grants from the Guggenheim Foundation, the National Endowment for the Arts, and the Whiting Foundation.

DENISE LEVERTOV was born in London, England, in 1923. She served as a nurse in World War II. Her first book of poems, *The Double Image,* was published in London in 1946. She came to the United States in 1948 and was naturalized in 1955. "I long for poems of an inner harmony in utter contrast to the chaos in which they exist," she wrote in 1959. "Insofar as poetry has a social function it is to awaken sleepers by other means than shock." In 1966 she was among the cofounders of American Writers Against the Vietnam War. For years she taught at Brandeis University part of the year and the other part at Stanford. In 1992, she retired from Stanford and moved to Seattle, where she lived until her death from lymphoma in December 1997. She wrote more than thirty collections of poetry, including *Collected Earlier Poems, 1940–1960* (1979), *Breathing the Water* (1987), *A Door in the Hive* (1989), and *Sands of the Well* (1996), all from New Directions. A volume entitled *This Great Unknowing: Last Poems* will be issued by the same publisher in 1999. Her work was selected for the 1990, 1993, and 1997 editions of *The Best American Poetry.*

PHILIP LEVINE was born in Detroit, Michigan, in 1928. For his writing he has received two Pulitzer Prizes, two National Book Awards, two National Book Critics Circle Awards, the Lenore Marshall Award, and the Ruth Lilly Award. His most recent books of poetry are *The Return* (1999), *The Simple Truth* (1994) and *What Work Is* (1991), all from

Knopf, and *Unselected Poems* (Greenhouse Review Press, 1997). In 1994 Knopf also published *The Bread of Time: Toward an Autobiography.* He teaches at New York University, and divides his time between New York and Fresno, California.

Of "The Return," Levine writes: "I believe the poem was born out of the experience of turning seventy, twice the age of my father when he died. During my years as a boy and a young man growing up in Detroit I went back again and again to places I knew he'd frequented in an effort to find some trace or hint of his nature. I must have failed, for I kept repeating the search. A few years ago my mother—knowing she was nearing the end (she was over ninety)—presented me with a thick packet of letters he'd written her in the late twenties and early thirties. Most of them were on hotel stationery from such cities as New York, Philadelphia, and Chicago where he'd gone repeatedly on business. It was the first time since he'd died in 1933 that I encountered his actual words and got a precise sense of how he expressed himself. To my surprise he was in the letters not the tall, austere, mysterious figure my memory had created out of the scraps of detail it contained; he was a man alone missing his home, his wife, his children. Did I ever make the actual trip I describe in the poem? No. The poem relies for its specificity on several other trips with the same or similar purposes, some real, some imagined."

DAVID MAMET was born in 1947. He is the author of numerous plays, including *Oleanna, Glengarry Glen Ross, American Buffalo,* and *Sexual Perversity in Chicago.* His films include *The Postman Always Rings Twice, The Verdict,* and *The Untouchables.* He was awarded the Pulitzer Prize in 1984. His first book of poems, *The Hero Pony,* was published by Grove Press in 1990. *The Chinaman,* a new collection, is forthcoming from Overlook Press. A novel entitled *Wilson* is scheduled to appear from Faber in February 2000. Asked how he manages to be so prolific in so many genres, Mamet replied, "I have no impulse control." He lives in Cambridge, Massachusetts.

GIGI MARKS was born in New York City in 1964. Her first collection of poems, *What We Need,* was published in March 1999, from Shortline Editions, a small press based in Minnesota. She teaches writing and literature at Hobart and William Smith Colleges, in Geneva, New York.

Marks writes: "Around the time I wrote 'The Swim,' I was returning to more regular work after being at home, raising two children, and I would often write at the kitchen table, after the kids were asleep, after I'd cleaned up, after I'd gone over a set of composition papers that I'd been grading; there would be this opportunity, and I'd write a poem or two. I'd been working over the same set of images in several poems, and 'The Swim' seems to me to be representative of this time; I'm pretty sure it was the last I wrote in this series. I had been spending a lot of my time in a very physical way—close to the children, often—and now I see the poems that I wrote then, 'The Swim' included, as tied to that particular kind of body knowledge: the language clear, the images concrete, the poems themselves compact—simple answers to complex questions."

WILLIAM MATTHEWS was born in Cincinnati, Ohio, in 1942. He graduated from Yale College in 1965 and received a master's degree a year later from the University of North Carolina at Chapel Hill. He went on to teach at Wells College, Cornell University, the University of Colorado, the University of Washington, and, beginning in 1983, the City College of New York. His book of poems, *Time and Money* (Houghton Mifflin, 1995), received the National Book Critics Circle Award in poetry. A book of translations, *The Mortal City: 100 Epigrams of Martial,* appeared from Ohio Review Books in 1995. At the time of his death, just after his fifty-fifth birthday, in November 1997, he had finished work on a manuscript of poems and on a translation of Horace's satires. He wrote passionately about jazz and elegiacally about jazz musicians in such early poems as "Blues for John Coltrane, Dead at 41," "Bud Powell, Paris, 1959," and "Listening to Lester Young." Here, from "Unrelenting Flood" in *Flood* (1983), is his riff on the near-blind Art Tatum at the piano: "Think how blind and near- /blind pianists range along/ their keyboards by clambering / over notes a sighted man / would notice to leave out, / by stringing it all on one / longing, the way bee-fingered, / blind, mountainous Art / Tatum did, the way we like / joy to arrive: in such / unrelenting flood the only / way we can describe it / is by music or another / beautiful abstraction, / like a ray of sunlight / in a child's drawing/ running straight to a pig's ear, / tethering us all to our star." Matthews could write with mordant wit. In "Inspiration," a late poem, he wrote:

> I hate
> poetry readings and the dreaded verb
> 'to share.' Let me share this knife with your throat,
> suggested Mack.

After All, his last book, was published posthumously in 1998.

WESLEY MCNAIR was born in Newport, New Hampshire, in 1941, and has always lived in northern New England. He has five collections of poetry, including the 1998 volume *Talking in the Dark,* from Godine. In 1997 Godine reprinted his two previous volumes of verse in one book entitled *The Town of No & My Brother Running.* He is the editor of *The Quotable Moose: A Contemporary Maine Reader* (University Press of New England, 1994) and has recently assembled a volume of selected poems, as well as a manuscript of essays about New England poets and poetry. A recipient of grants from the Rockefeller, Fulbright, and Guggenheim foundations, McNair has held a National Endowment for the Humanities Fellowship in literature and two National Endowment for the Arts fellowships in poetry. He directs the creative writing program at the Farmington campus of the University of Maine, and lives with his wife, Diane, in Mercer, Maine.

Of "The Characters of Dirty Jokes," McNair writes: "Like most people, I heard and told my first dirty jokes early in life. In fact, rehearsing and passing them on to others as an adolescent was my first experience in storytelling—an experience that had its influence on me as a writer. From their vernacular roughness and their irreverence toward polite society, I learned a certain way of 'speaking American,' which also included the delicacy of taking the listener into one's confidence for the private, shared moment an off-color story depends on. Dirty jokes showed me the value of timing, too, important in both storytelling and making poems. As for the content of those early stories, I see looking back that they gave me my first exposure to surrealistic juxtaposition. Never mind the claim that surrealism, having its origins in Europe, is alien to American narratives, and consider the joke cited in my poem about the man who has a baby elephant's trunk surgically attached to his penis and is embarrassed at the cocktail party when the hostess passes out peanuts.

"With my poem I pay tribute to dirty jokes—not only to the help they have given me as a writer, but to their oddly innocent view of our humanity."

CZESLAW MILOSZ was born in Szetejnie (Lithuania) in 1911. He grew up in Wilno, where he attended Catholic schools. He began to write poetry seriously in Paris in 1934 and worked clandestinely as a writer and editor for resistance publications during World War II. A member of the Socialist Party, Milosz joined the Polish diplomatic service when the war ended; following the suppression of the coalition government in 1951, however, he broke with the regime and settled in Paris. Since 1961 he has been professor of Slavic languages and literature at the University of California at Berkeley. He received the Nobel Prize in literature in 1980. He presented the Norton Lectures at Harvard in 1981–82. His nonfiction works include *The Captive Mind* (a book about Communism and intellectuals; Knopf, 1953), *Native Realm* (autobiography), and *Visions from San Francisco Bay* (1982). Milosz, who has translated the poetry of Zbigniew Herbert, has written several novels, including *The Seizure of Power* (1982) and *The Land of Ulro* (1984), both from Farrar, Straus & Giroux. His books of poetry include *Collected Poems* (Ecco, 1988) and *Provinces* (1991). *Road-Side Dog,* a gathering of prose poems, essays, and parables, appeared in 1998 (Farrar, Straus & Giroux). "A Ball" was written in Polish and was translated by the author in collaboration with Robert Hass.

Of "A Ball," Milosz writes: "An enormous granite ball can be seen in the archaeological museum in San Jose, Costa Rica. Presumably it is a work of local Indians, whose tribe does not exist any more. They were small people, practically pygmies. As the artifacts in the museum show, they knew only primitive tools. The poem thus resulted from meditation upon our incomprehensible human species and its enigmatic past."

JOAN MURRAY was born in New York City, grew up in the South Bronx, and taught at Lehman College. She now makes her home near Albany, New York. She is an arts consultant (currently for the New York State Council on the Arts) and the artist representative for the New York State Arts and Cultural Coalition, the legislative advocacy group. Her two new books are *Looking for the Parade* (Norton, 1999), which Robert Bly chose for the National Poetry Series, and *Queen of the Mist* (Beacon, 1999). *The Same Water* appeared in 1990 (Wesleyan University Press).

Murray writes: " *'From* Sonny's Hands' is part of a long meditation on the nature of beauty and intelligence, called 'Sonny's Face. Sonny's Hands.' It's about Sonny Ovitt, who works on the grounds crew at Yaddo and often drives the 4 P.M. run to Saratoga. On one such trip, when no one else came, he spoke with me about his life. I wrote the poem that night. The first part focuses on the joyful, jagged 'openness' of Sonny's missing teeth. The second part (in answer to his saying 'I gave up on intelligence and chose my hands') shows what hands know when they're not bound up by too much thought.

"Concerned that Sonny might be embarrassed by what I'd written, I spoke with him the next day. I'm grateful to him for his trust. Later, I sent him a tape of the poem and heard he played it for all the Yaddo work staff. I'm pleased that Robert Bly chose the last four stanzas, which relay one of the most poignant (and most personal) things anyone has ever told me."

SHARON OLDS was born in San Francisco in 1942. She teaches at New York University and helps run a writing workshop—now in its fourteenth year—in a state hospital for the severely physically challenged. Her most recent book, *The Wellspring* (1996), was published by Knopf, which will bring out her next collection, *Blood, Tin, Straw,* in the fall of 1999. She was appointed New York State Poet in 1998. She lives in New York City.

Of "What It Meant," Olds writes: "Around the time I wrote this, I had been reading Lucille Clifton (*The Book of Light*) and Charles Wright (*Black Zodiac*). Guided by their craft and art, I was thinking-without-thinking about religious experience, the life of the spirit, the sense of identity, and poetry.

"And maybe this poem 'began' in me (or signaled that it was done? needing only the translation from skillet to plate? Careful! Over easy!) when something in me respected ignorance and felt like honoring it. Until near the end of the first draft, I did not know where the poem was going."

The phrase "In the beauty of the lilies" is from "The Battle Hymn of the Republic."

MARY OLIVER was born in Ohio in 1935. She currently holds the Catharine Osgood Foster Chair for Distinguished Teaching at Bennington College. Her books of poetry include *American Primitive, Dream Work, House of Light, White Pine,* and *West Wind.* She has also published the essay collections *Blue Pastures* and *Winter Hours.* Her current publisher is Houghton Mifflin. She has received the Pulitzer Prize for *American Primitive,* the National Book Award for her *New and Selected Poems,* and a generous number of other recognitions. She lives in Provincetown, Massachusetts, and in Bennington, Vermont.

Oliver writes: " 'Flare' is one section of what will be, when finished, a long seven-part interconnected poem, which, in its entirety, will be called *The Leaf and the Cloud,* a phrase received from a John Ruskin quote. Working on this poem has been like swimming in the ocean instead of a pool, or even a mountain stream. More delight, more danger, more manipulation by the elements, and, sometimes, no shore in sight."

FRANCO PAGNUCCI was born in 1940 in Ruota, Italy, a twelfth-century village in the foothills of the Apennines an hour or two from Pisa and Florence. He grew up in a flat suburb an hour from Chicago. But there he found the Fox River to fish in and large fields to roam over. He arrived in Wisconsin in the late sixties to teach in the English Department of the University of Wisconsin–Platteville and has been there ever since: "Platteville is a small rural town not far from the Mississippi River; it's an unglaciated area with many hills. Maybe that's why I have felt at home here and have found much in the landscape to write about."

His publications include storytelling books: *Do Me! Stories* (1993) and *Storytelling Magic* (1997), both from Bur Oak Press. His books of poetry are *Face the Poem* (Bur Oak Press, 1979), *New Roads Old Towns* (Roundtree, 1988), *Out Harmsen's Way* (Fireweed Press, 1991), *I Never Had a Pet* (Bur Oak Press, 1992), and *Ancient Moves* (Bur Oak Press, 1998).

Pagnucci writes: " 'And Now' takes place in the lake country of northern Wisconsin, where the trees often remind me of the trees in the landscape of my boyhood in Italy. A friend who teaches birding here at the university believes people are, like birds, very much affected by imprinting of early images. So I am not surprised that for me poems come much easier and much more often in the outdoors. In the outdoors all that seems needed is to look and listen. The poems seem to come like leaves and flowers and fruits."

MOLLY PEACOCK was born in Buffalo, New York, in 1947 and lives both in London, Ontario, Canada, and New York City. She is the author of four books of poems, including *Original Love* (Norton, 1995), as well as a memoir, *Paradise Piece By Piece*. She was president of the Poetry Society of America from 1989 until 1994. Her most recent book is *How to Read a Poem and Start a Poetry Circle*. She is a contributing writer for Condé Nast's *House & Garden* and coeditor of *Poetry in Motion: 100 Poems from the Subways and Buses*.

Of "Say You Love Me," Peacock writes: "The first public exposure of 'Say You Love Me' occurred in the winter of 1987 when William Matthews invited me to speak to his class at Columbia University and, to tell you the truth, the whole class stared at the poem as if I had placed a turd on the table before them. Poor Bill Matthews said laconically, 'Well, the poem is very bald.' A *hairless* turd. He then tried a rescue, 'Molly,' he asked, 'how did you get to the word *burled*?' This makes me realize how often I have been saved by rhyme schemes.

"I occupy dangerous ground, the terrain of autobiography and formal design. The issue of how much of an 'I' should be in a poem would play out in Laurence Goldstein's decision to publish 'Say You Love Me' in the *Michigan Quarterly Review* in 1988, and then for me as I prepared to include the poem in my book *Take Heart* in 1989. In 1998, the editors Rebecca Wolf and Frances Richard asked to include 'Say You Love Me' in their remarkable new journal *Fence* (which proposes to explore the aesthetic issues in the boundaries between the least personal and the most personal American poetry). It accompanies an essay about the relationship of sound structures in poetry to trauma. Now the interrelationship of feeling and form, probably the oldest aesthetic issue, pulses at the cutting edge of poetry at the last edge of this century.

"When I heard that Robert Bly chose the poem for this volume, I e-mailed David Lehman to confess that it was not born yesterday. But the editors were amused by the determined reincarnating of this poem and so I tell you its story.

" 'I'm not a writer who uses the pronoun *I*,' a student in that workshop announced on the cold afternoon of the poem's debut slightly over ten years ago. Since then I have heard many poets say this, sometimes just as haughtily, sometimes as a cautionary phrase. Never have I heard that more than in 1999. *Oh dear,* I always think, *who else's experience belongs to me but mine?* Prosody also belongs to me, as rich with possibilities of expression as I could ever care to use. Structures of line, sound, and vocabulary, combined with the storyteller's art of delaying experience to replicate the terrible tensions of real time passing, let me make art of what happens to me, as I think in some way all poets have been doing since the days of cuneiform."

DAVID RAY was born in Oklahoma in 1932 and was educated at the University of Chicago. He now lives in Tucson and teaches at the University of Arizona. His many books include *Sam's Book* (Wesleyan University Press, 1987), *Wool Highways* (Helicon Nine Editions, 1993), *Kangaroo Paws* (Thomas Jefferson University Press, 1994), *HeartStones* (Micawber Fine Editions, 1998), and *Demons in the Diner* (Ashland Poetry Press, 1999). His many honors include two William Carlos Williams Awards from the Poetry Society of America, a National Endowment for the Arts Fellowship in fiction, and a Woursell Foundation Stipendium.

Ray writes: " 'Hemingway's Garden' is a selection from my book of poems about Ernest Hemingway. This poem touches on themes developed in the rest of the book, i.e. the writer's violence, marital problems, mental illness, and suicide. The problem with such tragic material is to

counterpoint it with enough humor to make it bearable. 'Heming-
way's Garden' was less of a challenge in this regard than were some of
the other poems in the manuscript dealing with Hemingway's partici-
pation in war crimes, his African bride, and his battles with himself, with
women, and with other literary figures. 'Hemingway's Garden,' then, is
what Hemingway himself might call the tip of an iceberg."

ADRIENNE RICH was born in 1929 in Baltimore, Maryland. She graduated
from Radcliffe College in 1951, the year her first book, *A Change of World*,
was chosen by W. H. Auden for the Yale Series of Younger Poets. She
was married from 1953 to 1970 and has three sons. Since 1976 she has
lived with the writer Michelle Cliff. She has published fourteen books
of poetry and four of prose, including *Blood, Bread and Poetry* (Norton,
1986) and *What Is Found There: Notebooks on Poetry and Politics* (Norton,
1993). "Seven Skins" appears in her most recent book of poems, *Midnight
Salvage* (Norton, 1999). For the past fifteen years she has lived in Cali-
fornia. She was the guest editor of *The Best American Poetry 1996*.

Rich writes: "What interests me about 'Seven Skins' is its tonal
movement from the coolly anecdotal to the ecstatic, a matter of voice,
primarily. There is a legend or folk tale (whence the title) about a
young woman who must spend the night with a serpent—actually a
transformed prince. She is told to dress in seven shifts and, whenever
the serpent bids her shed a shift, tells him: 'Serpent, shed a skin.' Of
course when the final skin is shed he is a naked man. There was actu-
ally a restaurant in Boston in the 1950s famed for its baked alaska
dessert served in a flowerpot, live tulip and all."

ALBERTO RÍOS was born in Nogales, Arizona, in 1952. He is the author
of seven books or chapbooks of poetry and two collections of short sto-
ries. His books of poems include *Teodoro Luna's Two Kisses* (Norton,
1990) and *The Curtain of Trees* (University of New Mexico, 1999). He
has received fellowships from the Guggenheim Foundation and the
National Endowment for the Arts. He is Regents' Professor of English
at Arizona State University.

Of "Writing from Memory," Ríos writes: "This poem's idea first
came to me at the Bread Loaf writers' conference, where I was teaching
several summers back. One night I went to dinner in the wonderfully
noisy dining hall. During a loud conversation about parents, I said
something to the effect that I did not resemble my father, who was very
dark-skinned, but rather my mother. I continued by saying that, like me,

she had a beard. Everyone burst into laughter. I of course meant that unlike me, she had no beard, but it somehow came out the opposite. This sometimes happens to all of us when we're talking. I was struck by the moment as I was thinking about it later, and was reminded that Tristan Tzara 'invented' Dada when he inadvertently stuck a brioche up his nose rather than into his mouth as he distractedly ate breakfast one morning. For him the world changed at that instant."

KAY RYAN was born in California in 1945 and grew up in the small towns of the San Joaquin Valley and the Mojave Desert. She studied at the Los Angeles and Irvine campuses of the University of California. Since 1971 she has lived in Marin County and has made her living teaching basic skills part-time at the College of Marin. She has published three books of poetry, *Flamingo Watching* (1994) and *Strangely Marked Metal* (1985), both from Copper Beech Press, and *Elephant Rocks* (Grove, 1996). She is a recipient of an Ingram Merrill Award and two Pushcart Prizes. Her work was included in *The Best American Poetry 1995* and *The Best of the Best American Poetry 1988–1997*.

Ryan writes: "I found my title, 'That Will to Divest,' in an essay by Milan Kundera. Kundera was saying something admiring about the modern composer Leoš Janáček, how Janáček was trying to write music in a new, denser way. But did I care? No. It was that single radiant—possibly radioactive—phrase that I loved. I don't know why writers go to such pains to make sense when somebody like me is just going to come along and read their work like a crow looking for shiny objects.

"It scares me how, as my poem begins, 'Action creates a taste for itself.' Among the various forces that can make us crazy, this is a big one; we are designed to go too far in any direction we're going in. I like simplifying. I like to think of this as a sterling virtue, but apparently it also worries me.

"I have just thought: rhyming is another action that creates a taste for itself. It must therefore also be possible to overdo rhymes. If this poem is a little too reduced and a little too rhymy, it proves its point."

SONIA SANCHEZ was born in Birmingham, Alabama, in 1934. She is the author of sixteen books, including *Homegirls and Handgrenades* (Thunder's Mouth Press, 1984), *Wounded in the House of a Friend* (Beacon, 1995), *Does Your House Have Lions?* (Beacon, 1997), *Like the Singing Coming Off the Drums* (Beacon, 1998) and *Shake Loose My Skin: New and Selected Poems* (Beacon, 1999). She has received a National Endowment for the Arts Fellowship, a PEN Fellowship in the arts, and a Governor's Award for excellence in humanities. *Does Your House Have Lions?* was a finalist for a National Book Critics Circle Award in 1998. She is Laura Cornell Professor of English at Temple University. She lives in Philadelphia.

Of "Last recording session/for papa joe," Sanchez writes: "This poem, published in *Under a Soprano Sky* in 1987 by Africa World Press, was written for Papa Joe Jones, the great African-American drummer. Papa Joe was giving a young musician a 'hard time' at this recording. All perfectionists know why he was doing this. All artists at the end of a career understand his intent! I wanted to put these feelings on paper to pay honor to this great musician who in his time outran the air with his incessant beat!"

REVAN SCHENDLER was born in New York City in 1965. She lived in Prague for four years. Now a student of oral history—interviewing Czechs about their memories of state socialism—and occasional teacher, she has also spent time as an editor, journalist, garden-book seller, and puppet costume maker. She lives in London.

MYRA SHAPIRO was born in the Bronx in 1932. She returned to New York after forty-five years in Georgia and Tennessee where she married, raised two daughters, and worked as a librarian and teacher of English. In 1993 she earned an MFA at Vermont College. She teaches poetry workshops under the auspices of the International Women's Writing Guild and serves on the board of directors of Poets House, a library and meeting place for poets, located in SoHo. Her book of poems, *I'll See You Thursday* (Blue Sofa Press), was published in 1996.

Shapiro writes: "I wrote 'Longing and Wonder' to hold on to a gift, to convey my happiness at receiving it: the words of the penultimate stanza. When they surfaced, I felt as wise as I'm ever likely to become. School situations have a way of tongue-tying us—what does the teacher want?—and there I was, a sixty-four-year-old poet with a first book, being questioned by a university department chairman. When the answer came out of my mouth at the instruction of my eyes, book and body were one! In graduate school I remember a professor who called such a confluence being on your gyroscope. The sensation was so good I, who love cities, had to shape it into something concrete."

CHARLES SIMIC was born in Belgrade, Yugoslavia, in 1938 and immigrated to the United States in 1954. Since 1967 he has published more than sixty books in this country and abroad. His latest poetry collections include *Walking the Black Cat, A Wedding in Hell,* and *Hotel Insomnia,* all from Harcourt Brace. He won the Pulitzer Prize in 1990 for his book of prose poems *The World Doesn't End.* Four volumes of his prose have appeared in the University of Michigan Press's Poets on Poetry series, most recently *The Unemployed Fortune-Teller* (1994) and *Orphan Factory* (1997). His latest book of poems is *Jackstraws* (1999). Awarded a MacArthur Fellowship in 1984, he was the guest editor of *The Best American Poetry 1992.* Since 1973 he has taught English at the University of New Hampshire.

Of "Barber College Haircut," Simic writes: "Yes, there were such places in New York forty years ago. I went to them for haircuts because they were the cheapest. It felt like they were still learning their moves, each little clip took a lifetime of careful deliberation, so I had plenty of time to think about things. I remember one haircut so bad, I was forced to spend my days in hiding and come out only late at night. For all I know, I may have been the first punker in the history of the world."

LOUIS SIMPSON was born in Jamaica, West Indies, in 1923. He immigrated to the United States at the age of seventeen. He studied at Columbia University, then served with the 101st Airborne Division on active duty in France, Holland, Belgium, and Germany. After the war he continued his studies at Columbia and at the Sorbonne. After receiving his Ph.D. at Columbia, he taught at Columbia, the University of California at Berkeley, and the State University of New York at Stony Brook. In 1964 he received the Pulitzer Prize in poetry for *At the End of the Open Road* (Wesleyan University Press, 1963). His other books of poems include *A Dream of Governors* (Wesleyan), *Collected Poems* (Paragon House, 1990), and *There You Are* (Story Line Press). His works of prose include *Three on the Tower: The Lives and Works of Ezra Pound, T. S. Eliot and William Carlos Williams* (William Morrow, 1975) and *A Company of Poets,* a book of critical essays (University of Michigan Press, 1981).

Simpson writes: " 'A Shearling Coat' is based on a news item I saw some years ago in *The New York Times.* I revised the last two lines many times—it seemed that they said either too little or too much. I have left it to the reader to have his or her own thoughts about the incident. The question, 'What you do that for?' is left hanging in the air. Poetry doesn't provide answers—it makes you wonder."

THOMAS R. SMITH was born in Chippewa Falls, Wisconsin, in 1948. His books of poetry include *Keeping the Star* (New Rivers Press, 1988) and

Horse of Earth (Holy Cow! Press, 1994). His selection of the Canadian poet Alden Nowlan, *What Happened When He Went to the Store for Bread* (Nineties Press, 1993), has recently gone into a second printing. He has subsidized his writing through various means, including migrant farm work and folksinging, but currently makes his living as a freelance writer and editor. He is an associate editor at Ally Press and poetry critic for the *Minneapolis Star Tribune*. He lives with his wife, the artist Krista Spieler, in River Falls, Wisconsin.

Of "Housewarming," Smith writes: " 'Housewarming' is what it appears to be—a fairly straightforward rendering of a dream. At age forty-eight, I had, for the first time in my life, committed that defining adult act: becoming a homeowner. The dream occurred in late October, a few weeks before the housewarming and two nights after the anniversary of my father's death. My father, who had died two years earlier, was much on my mind; with some shock, I realized I'd reached the age he was when he first bought a house. The dream suggested to me that not only the living support us when we feather a nest for body and soul. In indigenous cultures it's common practice to install in one's house a smaller structure, a 'spirit house,' in which to invite and feed ancestral visitors. The dream itself, and the poem that followed it, seemed to function as such a house, gathering the spirits of the dead and the living in my family.

"I have frequently employed dreams in my writing, though not every dream lends itself equally to poetic treatment. I was startled by the multisensory richness of this particular creation of the unconscious; the vivid physicality, rare in dreams—the raw, windy darkness and the stinging cold—gave me the scent of a poem. All of us have both 'big' and 'little' dreams; the former dive directly into the deep currents of our lives, while the latter meander on the shoreline of daily minutiae. Though the resulting poem came to only thirteen lines (far shorter than this rumination), I did not for a moment underestimate the size of the dream."

MARCIA SOUTHWICK was born in Boston in 1949. A graduate of Emerson College and the Iowa Writers' Workshop, she lives in Santa Fe and is married to the physicist Murray Gell-Mann. She teaches at the University of New Mexico. Southwick is the author of three volumes of poetry: *The Night Won't Save Anyone* (University of Georgia Press), *Why the River Disappears* (Carnegie Mellon University Press), and *A Saturday Night at the Flying Dog and Other Poems* (Oberlin College Press), which won the 1998 *Field* Poetry Prize. Her work is anthologized in *The Mor-*

row Anthology of Younger American Poets, New American Poets of the Nineties, and *The Pushcart Prize Anthology.*

Of "A Star Is Born in the Eagle Nebula," Southwick writes: "This is the third in a series of elegies written for the poet Larry Levis, my former husband of nine years. The first two elegies are about losing Larry. They describe his absence and the part of my past that his death cut away from me. My grief had turned Larry into a lifeless stranger. The time I wrote the third elegy, however, the complicated layers of sorrow had begun to strip away, and I could see again the familiar old Larry I had known and loved. He became a reference point—a distinct place in my life I could return to and dwell in. That sensation of the dead returning to life in memory, after a long and alienating absence, must be an integral part of the grieving process. When this poem first appeared in print, one of my close friends called me and said that his first reaction was, 'Wait until Larry reads this! He'll love it.' My friend also had been deeply saddened by Larry's death, but for a second, Larry was back, complete and listening. That's exactly what I felt when I wrote the poem."

WILLIAM STAFFORD was born in Hutchinson, Kansas, in 1914. He received the National Book Award for *Traveling through the Dark* (1962). *The Way It Is,* a volume of his selected poems, was published recently by Graywolf Press. He taught at Lewis and Clark College in Portland, Oregon, for thirty years. The prolific Stafford, a conscientious objector during World War II, began then his unswerving habit of writing before dawn each day. His books of critical prose, all available in the University of Michigan Press's Poets on Poetry series, include *Writing the Australian Crawl, You Must Revise Your Life,* and the posthumous *Crossing Unmarked Snow* (1998). He was named the poet laureate of Oregon in 1975. His poem "Tuned In Late One Night" (1982) begins with this stanza:

Listen—this is a faint station
left alive in the vast universe.
I was left here to tell you a message
designed for your instruction or comfort,
but now that my world is gone I crave
expression pure as all the space
around me: I want to tell what is . . .

Stafford died in his home in Oregon in 1993.

PEGGY STEELE was born in Dophan, Alabama, and now lives in Bowling Green, Kentucky, with her husband, Frank. Both are editors of *Plainsong Poetry Journal*. She recently retired from teaching at Western Kentucky University. Her poems have appeared in *Blue Sofa, The American Voice, Barnwood*, and *Number One;* her short stories in *Groundwater* and *Adena*.

Of "The Drunkard's Daughter," Steele writes: "My father had recently died when I had the experience this poem tells about. I was a student at the University of Alabama. My bereavement had a hard-knotted feel. My grief over his death couldn't come out because it got lost in the general misery I'd had over him since I was a child. He was alcoholic and my parents were divorced. The night I came in tipsy, the old depression and longing had come over me, all but drowning me. I had a vision of him walking home alone, drunk, from his bar. I felt how lonely he was. He had no job in our town. He was excluded from our community. Yet he was a clear-eyed, no-nonsense sort of man. When the repeated line of this poem came to me, it released some of the grief and rescued my father for me.

"I didn't realize that this experience might make a poem, though. I didn't know that the kind of lifeline that could come to a drowning person could make a poem. Years later, I was listening to a creaky tape of a poetry festival in Martin, Tennessee. I heard another poem about a man driving his parents home through the snow—and suddenly I knew. I knew, I knew! I jumped off my chair and wrote this little poem, and it has been a little kernel at the center of all the others I ever wrote."

RUTH STONE was born in Roanoke, Virginia, in 1915. She is a professor of English at SUNY-Binghamton. Her most recent books of poetry include *Second Hand Coat* and *Who Is the Widow's Muse*, both published by Yellow Moon Press, and *Simplicity*, published by Paris Press.

Of "A Moment," Stone writes: "I think I write most often from a parent's point of view, and yet I seldom write explicitly about my children. Perhaps because of our shared grief, we respect our distances, our emotional boundaries; our rights to feel unique. In this poem I am resigned to this isolation. Even with our children, we are only among them for a moment. I am silent with my own terrible knowledge of what time does to us all; our lives, which are necessarily enclosed, which necessarily exclude the vast amorphous other, as the heron seems to behave as if the field belongs to the heron. I am speaking of a moment of illumination, an awareness beyond the self, that came as a gift; a moment, which is all I can know of eternity."

LARISSA SZPORLUK was born in Ann Arbor, Michigan, in 1967. She teaches creative writing at Bowling Green State University in Ohio, where she lives with her husband, Carlo Celli, and their two children. Her first book, *Dark Sky Question,* won the Barnard New Women Poets Prize in 1997 and was published by Beacon Press in 1998. She recently completed her second collection, *Isolato.*

Of "Deer Crossing the Sea," Szporluk writes: "This poem might be a lesson in recycling. The first three lines are the only ones that survived the original draft (which was called "Gethsemane" and had no deer in it whatsoever). Then when I was pleased with the deer, the last seven lines felt weak and I completely cut out the Christ imagery (blood, arrows, agony, and so on) and tried to create a 'waftier' close. Never has a poem of mine been so thoroughly transmogrified."

DIANE THIEL was born in Coral Gables, Florida, in 1967. She completed her BA and MFA at Brown University in 1990. She also studied at the Wilhelm Pieck Universität in Rostock, East Germany, in 1987. She teaches at the University of Miami and serves as a poet-in-residence for the Miami Book Fair's Poet in the Schools Program. She has received the Robinson Jeffers Prize for poetry, the Judith Siegel Pearson Award for poetry, and the Hackney Literary Award for the short story. Her chapbook, *Cleft in the Wall,* was released by Aralia Press in 1999. "The Minefield" will be published in a single-poem chapbook series by Aralia Press. *Writing Your Rhythm,* her writing guide, is forthcoming from Story Line Press.

Thiel writes: " 'The Minefield' is a central poem in a manuscript near completion. Several of the poems in the work deal with the question of lineage, the way history passes from our parents' hands into our own. In 1987, I participated in Brown University's exchange program with Rostock, East Germany. Visiting the places of my father's lost childhood helped me begin to understand the forces that had shaped him and had gone on to shape me. Some of the poems conceived as ideas in that experience have taken years to mature. I have a keener sense of history now, of the torches that have been passed to us, and of how we might choose to carry them ."

DAVID WAGONER was born in 1926 in Massillon, Ohio, and grew up in Whiting, Indiana. He is currently professor of English at the University of Washington, and the editor of *Poetry Northwest.* He has published fifteen books of poems and ten novels. His most recent book, *Traveling*

Light: Collected and New Poems, was published by the University of Illinois Press in 1999.

Of "Thoreau and the Crickets," Wagoner writes: "The poem is based on an incident described in Thoreau's *Journal.* It seemed to me like an experience I wanted to have myself, and so I wrote a poem about it."

RICHARD WILBUR was born in New York City in 1921. He attended Amherst and Harvard, and during World War II served with the 36th Infantry Division in Italy, France, and Germany. During 1987–88, he served as the second official poet laureate of the U.S., succeeding Robert Penn Warren. In 1989 he received a second Pulitzer Prize for *New and Collected Poems.* Prior to his retirement from teaching in 1986, he had taught at Harvard, Wellesley, Wesleyan, and Smith. His translations from Molière and Racine are frequently produced in the English-speaking world, and the musical show *Candide,* for which he wrote most of the lyrics, has most recently been revived (1999) by London's National Theatre. A late publication is *The Disappearing Alphabet* (Harcourt, 1998), a book for children and amusable adults. A new book of poems, *A Wall in the Woods,* is forthcoming, and he is at work on a translation of Molière's first full-length verse comedy, *L'Étourdi.* He and his wife live in Cummington, Massachusetts, and Key West, Florida.

Of "This Pleasing Anxious Being," Wilbur writes: "I think that people resist as long as they can a full sense of the world's change and of their own aging. At last, when a certain number of irreplaceable people are gone, and the home place has been razed, and one is the only rememberer of certain things, the gut acknowledges what the mind has always thought it knew. That is the source of this poem, which moves both back and forward in time, and considers time in a number of perspectives. The title is taken from the twenty-second stanza of Gray's 'Elegy.' "

C. K. WILLIAMS was born in Newark, New Jersey, in 1936 and was educated at the University of Pennsylvania. He teaches at Princeton University one semester a year, and lives the rest of the time in Paris. His most recent poetry books include *Flesh and Blood* (1987), *Poems 1963–1983* (1988), *A Dream of Mind* (1992), *The Vigil* (1996), and *Repair* (1999), all from Farrar, Straus & Giroux. *Flesh and Blood* won the National Book Critics Circle Award for 1987. In 1993, Williams received a Lila Wallace–Reader's Digest Writer's Award. He has translated Sophocles and Euripides. *Poetry and Consciousness,* a book of essays, appeared in the University of Michigan Press's Poets on Poetry series in 1998. In 2000 a book of his love poems, *Love Poems and Poems about Love,* will be published, as will a prose memoir, *Mourning.*

Williams writes: "What happened in 'Archetypes' happened and then a long time, nearly twenty years, later, I was finally able to figure out what that utterly ordinary and singularly strange moment which has so struck me had actually meant to me. I was relieved it arrived as a poem about love rather than terror, about intimacy rather than isolation."

CHARLES WRIGHT was born in Pickwick Dam, Tennessee, in 1935. Educated at Davidson College, he served in the army for four years, then attended the Writers' Workshop at the University of Iowa. He lectured at the universities of Rome and Padua under the Fulbright program. He has received fellowships from the National Endowment for the Arts and the Guggenheim Foundation and won a PEN Award for his translation of Eugenio Montale's *The Storm and Other Things.* He is a professor of English at the University of Virginia at Charlottesville, where he lives with his family. In 1996 the Lenore Marshall poetry prize was awarded to him for his book *Chickamauga* (1995). For *Black Zodiac* (Farrar, Straus & Giroux, 1997) he received the *Los Angeles Times* Book Prize, the National Book Critics Circle Award in poetry, and the Pulitzer Prize. *Appalachia* appeared in 1998. These three recent books will be published, with a seven-poem coda, in 2000 under the title *Negative Blue.*

Wright says: " 'American Twilight' is one of a series of poems leading up to the end of a book—and leading up to the final diminishment of everything. *Appalachia* should have been a Paradiso but it turned out to be a Book of the Dead. The character has come to the end of things, is about to enter the other side of things, and the speaker in the book is trying to help him along by whispering in his ear, as you do in a Book of the Dead."

TIMOTHY YOUNG was born in St. Paul, Minnesota, in 1949 and was educated at the University of Minnesota. His first book of poetry, *Men Don't Dance in America,* was published in 1984, and in 1985 he won the Lake Superior Contemporary Writers' Award. His newest collection, *Building in Deeper Water,* which includes "The Thread of Sunlight," will be published by Holy Cow! Press. Currently, he teaches juvenile offenders at the Minnesota Correctional Facility School in Red Wing, Minnesota. He lives in rural Wisconsin with his wife and sons.

Of "The Thread of Sunlight," Timothy Young writes: "Shortly after moving to the country, my wife and I squabbled about whether or not we should bug-bomb the old farmhouse. I felt an intense affection for the spiders, and couldn't answer when my wife asked 'Why?' I wrote 'The Thread of Sunlight' to answer her question.

"The poem takes place in the family lake cabin. I was about ten; it was 1960. Stories of duty to church and government were part of our family culture. It wasn't until six or seven years later that my parents began to talk about Vietnam. Mostly we talked about the work that needed to be done.

"Looking back, I see that beings such as spiders, bacteria, wild turkeys, and sheepdogs have guided me toward moments of unexpected illumination and new ways of living. I'm always surprised and grateful, and sometimes frightened."

MAGAZINES WHERE THE POEMS
WERE FIRST PUBLISHED

Acorn, ed. Susan Pagnucci. c/o Bur Oak Press, 8717 Mockingbird Road, Platteville, WI 53818.

AGNI, ed. Askold Melnyczuk. Boston University, 236 Bay State Road, Boston, MA 02215.

Alkali Flats, poetry ed. Jim Harrison. Montana State University–Billings, P.O. Box 50, 1500 N. 30th Street, Billings, MT 59101.

American Poetry Review, eds. Stephen Berg, David Bonanno, and Arthur Vogelsgang. 1721 Walnut Street, Philadelphia, PA 19103.

The Antioch Review, poetry ed. Judith Hall. P.O. Box 148, Yellow Springs, OH 45387.

The Atlantic Monthly, poetry ed. Peter Davison. 77 North Washington St., Boston, MA 02114.

The Bitter Oleander, ed. Paul B. Roth. 4983 Tall Oaks Dr., Fayetteville, NY 13066-9776.

Black Warrior Review, poetry ed. Matt Doherty. P.O. Box 862936, Tuscaloosa, AL 35486-0027.

Blasts! P.O. Box 40478, San Francisco, CA 94140.

Blue Sofa, ed. Nils Peterson. 418 California Street, Campbell, CA 95008.

The Café Review, ed. Steve Luttrell. c/o Yes Books, 20 Danforth Street, Portland, ME 04101.

Common Sense, ed. Michael Cummings. University of Notre Dame, P.O. Box 957, Notre Dame, IN 46556.

Conjunctions, ed. Bradford Morrow. Bard College, Annandale-on-Hudson, NY 12504.

Crab Orchard Review, poetry ed. Allison Joseph. English Dept., Faner Hall, Southern Illinois University at Carbondale, Carbondale, IL 62901-4503.

Cream City Review, poetry eds. Laura Micciche and Karen Howland. P.O. Box 413, Dept. of English, University of Wisconsin, Milwaukee, WI 53201.

DoubleTake, poetry ed. Edward Hirsch. 1317 West Pettigrew Street, Durham, NC 27705.

Fence, poetry eds. Caroline Crumpacker and Matthew Rohrer. 14 Fifth Ave., #1A, New York, NY 10011.

Figdust, eds. Suzi Sheffield and Brennan Collins. P.O. Box 789, Athens, GA 30603.

The Gettysburg Review, ed. Peter Stitt. Gettysburg College, Gettysburg, PA 17325.

Green Mountains Review, poetry ed. Neil Shepard. Johnson State College, Johnson, VT 05656.

Hambone, ed. Nathaniel Mackey, 134 Hunolt Street, Santa Cruz, CA 95060.

Harvard Review, poetry ed. David Rivard. Poetry Room, Harvard College Library, Cambridge, MA 02138.

The Hudson Review, eds. Paula Deitz and Frederick Morgan. 684 Park Avenue, New York, NY 10021.

The Journal of Family Life, ed. Ellen Becker. 22 Elm Street, Albany, NY 12202.

Kalliope, ed. Mary Sue Koeppel. Florida Community College, 3939 Roosevelt Blvd., Jacksonville, FL 32205.

Literal Latté, ed. Jenine Gordon Bockman. 61 East Eighth Street, Suite 240, New York, NY 10003.

Many Mountains Moving, eds. Naomi Horii and Marilyn Krysl. 420 22nd Street, Boulder, CO 80302.

Meridian, ed. Ted Genoways. Dept. of English, University of Virginia, Charlottesville, VA 22903.

Mid-American Review, poetry ed. David Hawkins. Dept. of English, Bowling Green State University, Bowling Green, OH 43403.

The New England Review, ed. Stephen Donadio. Middlebury College, Middlebury, VT 05753.

New Millennium Writings, ed. Don Williams. P.O. Box 2463, Knoxville, TN 37901.

The New Yorker, poetry ed. Alice Quinn. 20 West 43rd Street, New York, NY 10036.

Ontario Review, ed. Raymond J. Smith. 9 Honey Brook Drive, Princeton, NJ 08540.

Painted Bride Quarterly, eds. Kathy Volk Miller and Marion Wrenn. 230 Vine Street, Philadelphia, PA 19106.

Partisan Review, poetry ed. Rosanna Warren. 236 Bay State Road, Boston, MA 02215.

Paterson Literary Review, ed. Maria Mazziotti Gillan. Passaic County Community College, One College Boulevard, Paterson, NJ 07505-1179.

Ploughshares, eds. Don Lee and David Daniel. Emerson College, 100 Beacon Street, Boston, MA 02116.

Poetry, ed. Joseph Parisi. 60 West Walton Street, Chicago, IL 60610-3380.

Poetry Daily, eds. Rob Anderson, Diane Boller, and Don Selby. www.poems.com.

Potomac Review, ed. Eli Flam. P.O. Box 354, Port Tobacco, MD 20677.

The Progressive, ed. Matthew Rothschild. 409 East Main Street, Madison, WI 53703.

The Prose Poem, ed. Peter Johnson. English Dept., Providence College, 549 River Avenue, Providence, RI 02918-0001.

River City, ed. Paul Naylor. English Department, University of Memphis, Memphis, TN 38152.

Rosebud, ed. Rod Clark. P.O. Box 459, Cambridge, WI 53523.

Salmagundi, ed. Robert Boyers. Skidmore College, Saratoga Springs, NY 12866.

Seneca Review, ed. Deborah Tall. Hobart and William Smith Colleges, Geneva, NY 14456-3397.

The Sewanee Review, ed. George Core. University of the South, Sewanee, TN 37383-1000.

Shenandoah, ed. R. T. Smith. Troubadour Theater, 2nd Floor, Washington and Lee University, Lexington, VA 24450-0303.

Solo, eds. David Oliveira and Jackson Wheeler. Solo Press, 5146 Foothill Road, Carpinteria, CA 93013.

The Southern Review, poetry eds. James Olney and Dave Smith. 43 Allen Hall, Louisiana State University, Baton Rouge, LA 70803.

Tor House Newsletter, ed. Jackie Baumann. 14A Sunset Center, P.O. Box 2713, Carmel, CA 93921.

Verse, eds. Brian Henry and Andrew Zawacki. c/o Henry, English Dept., Plymouth State College, Plymouth, NH 03264.

Water Stone, ed. Mary Rockcastle. Graduate Liberal Studies Program, Hamline University, 1536 Hewitt Ave., St. Paul, MN 55104-1284.

The Yale Review, ed. J. D. McClatchy. P.O. Box 208243, New Haven, CT 06520-8243.

ACKNOWLEDGMENTS

The series editor thanks his assistant, Mark Bibbins, for his invaluable work on this book. Warm thanks go also to Glen Hartley and Lynn Chu of Writers' Representatives, and to Gillian Blake, Erich Hobbing, Joy Jacobs, and Giulia Melucci of Scribner.

Grateful acknowledgment is made to the publications from which the poems in this volume were chosen. Unless specifically noted otherwise, copyright to the poems is held by the individual poets.

Dick Allen: "The Selfishness of the Poetry Reader" appeared in *The Café Review*. Reprinted by permission of the poet.

John Balaban: "Story" from *Locusts at the Edge of Summer* by John Balaban. Copyright © 1999 by John Balaban. First appeared in *Verse*. Reprinted by permission of the poet and Copper Canyon Press.

Coleman Barks: "Bill Matthews Coming Along (1942–1997)" appeared in *Figdust*. Reprinted by permission of the poet.

George Bilgere: "Catch" appeared in *Sewanee Review*. Reprinted by permission of the poet.

Elizabeth Bishop: "Foreign-Domestic" appeared in *Conjunctions*. Copyright © 1998 by the Estate of Elizabeth Bishop. Reprinted with the permission of Farrar, Straus & Giroux.

Chana Bloch: "Tired Sex" appeared in *The Atlantic Monthly*. Reprinted by permission of the poet.

Philip Booth: "Narrow Road, Presidents' Day" appeared in *American Poetry Review*. Reprinted by permission of the poet.

John Brehm: "Sea of Faith" appeared in *The Southern Review*. Reprinted by permission of the poet.

Hayden Carruth: "Because I Am" appeared in *Seneca Review*. Reprinted by permission of the poet.

Lucille Clifton: "the mississippi river empties into the gulf" appeared in *The Terrible Stories*. Copyright © 1996 by Lucille Clifton. Later reprinted in *River City*. Reprinted by permission of the poet and BOA Editions Ltd.

Billy Collins: "Dharma" first appeared in *Poetry*. Copyright © 1998 by Billy Collins. Reprinted by permission of the poet and the editor of *Poetry*.

Robert Creeley: "Mitch" from *Life and Death*. Copyright © 1998 by Robert Creeley. Reprinted by permission of the poet and New Directions Publishing Corp. First appeared in *Solo*.

Lydia Davis: "Betrayal" appeared in *Hambone*. Reprinted by permission of the poet.

Debra Kang Dean: "Taproot" from *News of Home*. Copyright © 1998 by

ALSO AVAILABLE FROM
THE BEST AMERICAN POETRY SERIES